THE
INTERNATIONAL
DESSERT BOOK

THE INTERNATIONAL DESSERT BOOK

Goldye Mullen

Illustrated by

Ten Speed Press

© 1979 Goldye Mullen
Library of Congress Catalog Number 79-1726
THE INTERNATIONAL DESSERT BOOK is published by Ten Speed Press, Box 7123, Berkeley, CA 94707
ISBN 0-913668-75-3 paper $7.95; ISBN 0-913668-74-5 cloth $10.95
Printed in The United States of America

I dedicate this book to my daughters,
Judith and Temmy
and to my husband, Edward.
They are the sweetness in my life.

A Word About the Past and a Taste of Things to Come:

The old familiar cry, "what's for dessert, mom?" is a question close to my heart. As a child, it was the first question I asked when we sat down to dinner. In restaurants I looked at the bottom of the menu first, where desserts are listed, and then glanced upward.

As a home economist, it is obvious that I would have an interest in food. However, my desire to prepare and present attractive and inviting dishes goes beyond my academic background. During my husband's career with the Government we entertained frequently and invariably I decided in the dessert first and the entree second.

These recipes have been gathered from family, friends, official Washington, D.C., and in our travels to England, Ireland, Scandinavia, Holland, Belgium, Switzerland, Austria, France, Israel, Greece, Spain, Portugal, and Guatemala. People were very gracious about giving me recipes.

Menus from different countries are fun and challenging to prepare. A party planned with an entire menu from one country or one having each course from a different country is always a huge success. Invariably, the conversation centers around recollections of travels or personal experiences with ethnic cooking and these stories become part of the delightful repast.

Enjoy!

Contents

Refrigerated Desserts

Contents

*R*efrigerator desserts are a boon for a cook since preparations may be done ahead of time; but remember, when you are serving a frozen fruit dessert, let it thaw before serving by moving it from the freezer to the main part of the refrigerator when you sit down to dinner, and it should be just right when you are ready to serve it.

And don't forget

- Egg whites may be folded into a hot sauce or batter. Unlike whipped cream, which will liquefy when put in hot ingredients, egg whites are not affected.
- Because chocolate burns easily, take care when it is melting. Break the chocolate into small pieces, place in small saucepan, and set pan over very hot but not simmering water. Stir constantly until chocolate is melted.
- Egg yolks should not be overbeaten with sugar or they will become granular. Add sugar gradually and beat until mixture is pale yellow and thick enough so that when a small amount is lifted in the beater it will fall back into the bowl.
- Whipped cream can be kept in the refrigerator for several hours. A small amount of liquid may be exuded, which should not be used.
- Heavy cream doubles and often triples in volume when whipped.
- One egg white equals 2 tablespoons; egg whites may be frozen in a covered jar.
- Whipped cream folded into other ingredients will thin out and lose its stiffness if other ingredients are not cold.
- Yolks in light custard sauces can be prevented from scrambling by using a small amount of starch as a safeguard.

Refrigerator Mocha Torte

*1 two-layer
    sponge cake*

1/4 cup crème de cacao

1 pint heavy cream

1-1/2 tablespoons cocoa

*1-1/2 tablespoons
    instant coffee*

*1 pint thick commercial
    fudge sauce*

1/2 cup slivered almonds

1. Any 8-inch sponge cake recipe or a commercially prepared cake may be used. Split to make four layers.

2. Place layer on large plate and sprinkle with 1 tablespoon crème de cacao.

3. Whip cream and mix in cocoa and coffee.

4. Spread fudge sauce over layer sprinkled with crème de cacao. Over that spread whipped cream mixture.

5. Place second layer on top and repeat with crème de cacao, fudge sauce and whipped cream. Do same with third layer.

6. Top with last layer and cover sides and top with remainder of whipped cream. Refrigerate overnight.

7. Just before serving, garnish top and sides with almonds.

Yield: 8-10 servings

Crème des Oranges et Abricots

1/2 pound dried apricots

1 medium orange

1/2 cup sugar

1/4 cup coarsely chopped walnuts

1/4 cup kirsch or any orange flavored liqueur

1/2 pint heavy cream, whipped

1 square bitter chocolate

1. Place apricots in a saucepan and cover with cold water. Allow to soak for several hours or overnight until soft.

2. Chop entire orange, pulp and rind in a blender. Add, with sugar, to apricots.

3. Cook apricots over very low heat until tender and most of liquid is absorbed. This should take about 15 minutes.

4. When mixture is cool, blend in a blender or rub through a sieve as soon as it is removed from heat and cool afterwards.

5. Stir in nuts and liqueur. Fold in whipped cream.

6. Grate chocolate and sprinkle over top.

Yield: 6 servings

This may be served either from a large crystal bowl at the table or as individual servings in *pots de crème*, with grated chocolate sprinkled over each one.

Almond Cake Roll

4 egg yolks

3/4 cup sugar

1-1/2 teaspoons almond
   extract

2 tablespoons water

4 egg whites

3/4 cup cake flour

1 teaspoon baking
   powder

1/4 teaspoon salt

4 ounces finely
   chopped blanched
   almonds

Preheat oven to 375°.

1. Beat egg yolks until thick and lemon-colored. Gradually beat in half the sugar. (Reserve other half of sugar for egg whites.)

2. Blend in almond flavoring and water.

3. Beat egg whites until soft peaks form. Then using about 2 tablespoons at a time, gradually beat in remaining sugar.

4. Carefully fold beaten egg whites into yolk mixture.

5. Sift together cake flour, baking powder, and salt. Stir in chopped nuts.

6. Using about one quarter cup at a time, carefully fold dry mixture into egg batter. Make certain that mixture is thoroughly blended.

7. Line a 10 x 15 x ½-inch jellyroll pan with well-greased waxed paper. Spread mixture evenly. Bake at 375° for about 15 minutes. When cake is finished, turn out onto a towel dusted with confectioners' sugar. Strip off waxed paper and quickly roll cake up like a jelly roll. Then wrap the whole roll in another towel and allow to cool until near serving time. Then make filling and follow directions below for finishing.

CREAM FILLING

1 pint heavy cream

1/2 cup confectioners' sugar

1 teaspoon vanilla

toasted slivered almonds

1. Just before serving, whip cream until it begins to thicken, add sugar, and whip until stiff.

2. Mix in vanilla. Unroll the cake and fill it with half of the whipped cream. Then gently roll it up again and spread the outside with remaining cream.

3. Garnish roll with almonds and serve.

Yield: makes 10 one-inch slices.

If you are planning to serve the cake roll for a party, the cake can be prepared days in advance and kept in the refrigerator, rolled in a towel with waxed paper around the towel to prevent drying.

The filling can be prepared just before you start your dinner and kept in a bowl in the refrigerator ready to be spread on the cake at serving time.

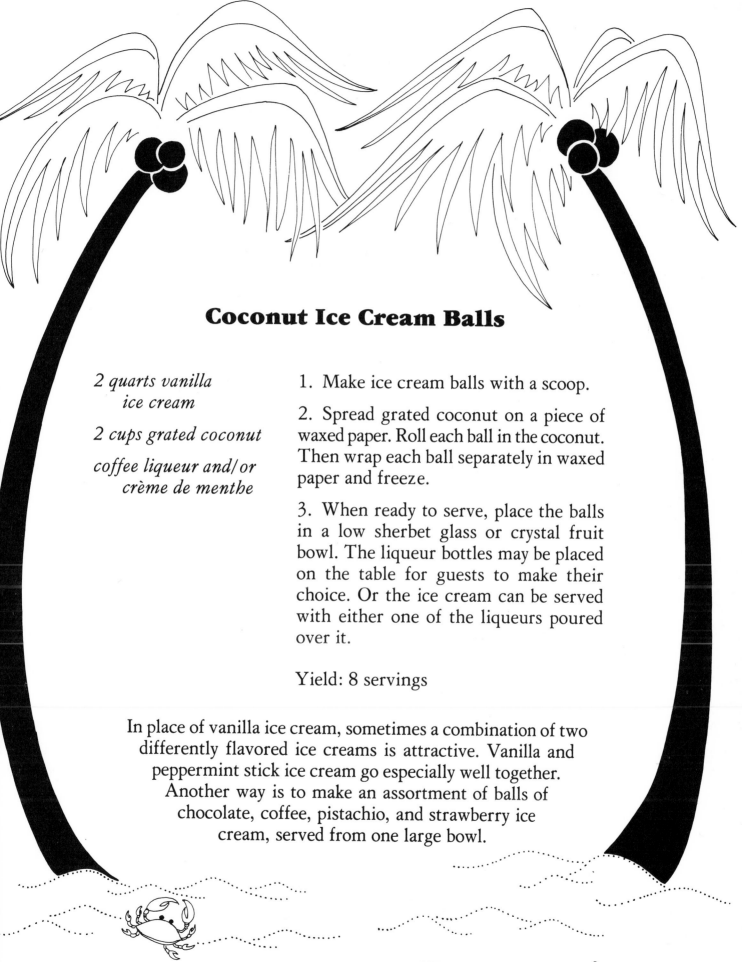

Coconut Ice Cream Balls

2 quarts vanilla
   ice cream

2 cups grated coconut

coffee liqueur and/or
   crème de menthe

1. Make ice cream balls with a scoop.

2. Spread grated coconut on a piece of waxed paper. Roll each ball in the coconut. Then wrap each ball separately in waxed paper and freeze.

3. When ready to serve, place the balls in a low sherbet glass or crystal fruit bowl. The liqueur bottles may be placed on the table for guests to make their choice. Or the ice cream can be served with either one of the liqueurs poured over it.

Yield: 8 servings

In place of vanilla ice cream, sometimes a combination of two differently flavored ice creams is attractive. Vanilla and peppermint stick ice cream go especially well together. Another way is to make an assortment of balls of chocolate, coffee, pistachio, and strawberry ice cream, served from one large bowl.

Chocolate Icebox Cake Supreme

24 ladyfingers

1/2 pound semisweet chocolate

3 tablespoons water

3 tablespoons confectioners' sugar

2 egg yolks

1/2 cup chopped walnut meats

2 egg whites

1 pint heavy cream

———

1/2 pint heavy cream

1 tablespoon confectioners' sugar

1 teaspoon vanilla

1. Split ladyfingers and arrange some on bottom of a lightly greased 9-inch spring form. Then place more ladyfingers, cut side in, upright and close together around the sides.

2. Melt chocolate in top of a double boiler. Remove from heat, add the water, and blend in. When chocolate is smooth, stir in the sugar and allow to cool.

3. Add egg yolks, one at a time, beating vigorously until smooth.

4. Fold in chopped nuts.

5. Beat egg whites stiff and fold into chocolate mixture. Whip cream stiff and carefully fold into chocolate mixture.

6. Spoon some of chocolate mixture over bottom layer of ladyfingers. Cover with another layer of ladyfingers and continue alternating between filling and ladyfingers. Plan your cake so that the top is a layer of ladyfingers. Use generous amounts of chocolate filling in the layers so that texture will be moist. Cover with waxed paper and refrigerate overnight.

7. When ready to serve, whip ½ pint heavy cream stiff. Mix in sugar and vanilla and spread over top.

Yield: 12-15 servings.

Chocolate Mousse

1/2 pound semisweet
  chocolate

1/2 ounce unsweetened
  chocolate

1/4 cup strong coffee

1/4 pound softened
  sweet butter

5 egg yolks

1/4 cup sugar

3 tablespoons
  orange liqueur

5 egg whites

pinch of salt

1 tablespoon sugar

1. In the top of a double boiler over hot water, melt chocolate and add coffee. Stir until mixture is blended and velvety.

2. Remove pan from heat and beat in butter, a little at a time until it is smooth as cream.

3. Beat yolks and sugar until mixture is pale yellow. Blend in the liqueur. Continue to beat until consistency of sour cream. Then beat chocolate into egg mixture.

4. Beat egg whites and salt until soft peaks form. Then add sugar and beat until stiff.

5. Fold beaten egg whites into chocolate mixture, gently but thoroughly.

6. Pour into serving dish or dessert glasses and chill for six to eight hours or overnight.

Yield: 6 to 8 servings

Chocolate Peppermint Glacé

CRUST

1/2 pound vanilla wafers

3 tablespoons sugar

4 tablespoons melted butter

1. Make crumbs in blender or roll wafers with rolling pin. Mix in sugar.

2. Mix melted butter with crumbs. Line a refrigerator tray with half the crumbs, reserving remainder for topping.

FILLING

1/2 cup butter

2 cups confectioners' sugar

2 tablespoons cocoa

2 egg yolks

1/2 teaspoon peppermint flavor

1 cup chopped walnuts

2 egg whites

1/4 teaspoon salt

1/2 pint heavy cream

1. Cream butter. Add powdered sugar and cocoa and blend well.

2. Beat egg yolks and stir into butter mixture.

3. Fold in peppermint flavor and chopped nuts.

4. Beat egg whites and salt until stiff and fold into above mixture.

5. Whip cream and gently blend through filling.

6. Turn into tray with crust and cover with remainder of crumbs. Chill 24 hours and when ready to serve, cut into squares.

Yield: 6 servings

Emperor's Dessert
(Kiwi Fruit Roma)

ICED SOUFFLÉ GLACÉ

10 ounces heavy cream

3 tablespoons sugar

3 tablespoons water

2 egg yolks

3/4 ounce rum

3 whole Kiwi fruits

rum

1. Whip heavy cream until stiff and set aside.

2. Heat sugar and water until dissolved. Beat egg yolks and add warm syrup. Continue to whip until stiff.

3. Carefully fold egg yolk mixture into whipped cream. Blend in rum.

4. If freezer space permits, fill 6 wine goblets 1/3 full and freeze. Otherwise, pour into a bowl and freeze.

5. Peel and thinly slice Kiwi fruit, place in shallow bowl and cover with rum. Chill until ready to serve. To serve, arrange rum flavored Kiwi slices around individual servings, top with Sabayon Sauce and serve immediately.

SABAYON SAUCE

2 egg yolks

1/4 cup confectioners' sugar

1/3 cup rum

1. Preferably in a copper bowl, beat egg yolks and sugar over warm water.

2. Add rum and continue to beat until it thickens. Serve hot or cold.

Yield: 6 servings

Emperor and Empress Hirohito of Japan visited San Francisco in 1975 and stayed at the St. Francis Hotel. Pastry Chef Otto Eckstein created this dessert for the State luncheon held at the hotel. It is delicate in flavor and beautiful to behold. Chef Eckstein explained that strawberries or blueberries could be substituted, however in that case sherry would be more appropriate.

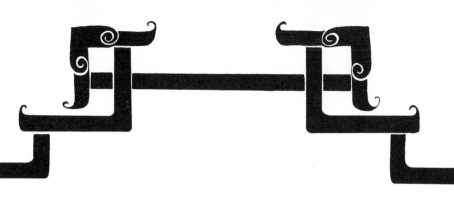

CHINESE SUNDAES

1 eleven-ounce can
   mandarin orange
   sections

1 tablespoon cornstarch

1 cup crushed
   pineapple, undrained

3/8 cup orange
   marmalade

1/4 teaspoon
   ground ginger

1/2 cup kumquat
   preserves

vanilla ice cream or
   lemon sherbet

1. Drain and reserve syrup from orange sections.

2. In a saucepan blend cornstarch with ¼ cup drained syrup.

3. To the above syrup mixture, add the undrained pineapple, marmalade and ginger. Stir well and cook over medium heat until the mixture begins to thicken, stirring constantly.

4. Blend in kumquat preserves and mandarin orange sections.

Yield: 2½ cups sauce

This sauce may be served warm or cold and may be made ahead of time and warmed up just before serving over ice cream or sherbet.

Fromage à la Crème

1 eight-ounce package
    cream cheese

2 tablespoons
    light cream

3 tablespoons
    confectioners' sugar

sprinkle of salt

1/2 pint heavy cream,
    whipped

1 tablespoon grated
    orange rind

fresh or frozen berries

1. Keep cheese at room temperature until soft and then blend in cream, sugar and salt.

2. Fold in whipped cream and orange rind.

3. Line a quart mold with double thickness cheese cloth which has been rung out in ice water. Allow one inch to hang over sides. Pour in mixture and refrigerate overnight.

4. When ready to serve, unmold and peel off cheese cloth. Serve with any sugared fresh berries as a topping or thawed and drained frozen berries.

Another garnish is raspberry sauce.

RASPBERRY SAUCE

1/4 cup sugar

2 teaspoons cornstarch

1 tablespoon brandy

1 ten-ounce package
    frozen raspberries,
    thawed

1. Blend sugar, cornstarch and brandy.

2. Stir sugar mixture into thawed raspberries and cook over moderate heat, stirring constantly until mixture thickens and clears.

3. Cool before serving.

Yield: 8 servings

Frosted Lemon Pie

CRUST

1-1/4 cups graham
    cracker crumbs

1/3 cup sugar

1 teaspoon cinnamon

1/3 cup melted butter
    or margarine

1. Blend crumbs, sugar, and cinnamon.

2. Mix melted fat into crumbs.

3. Line a refrigerator tray with waxed paper and spread two-thirds of the crumb mixture on the bottom.

FILLING

1 egg

2 egg yolks

1/2 cup sugar

1/4 teaspoon salt

1/4 cup strained
    lemon juice

1 teaspoon grated
    lemon rind

2 egg whites

1/2 pint heavy cream

1 tablespoon
    confectioners' sugar

1. In top of double boiler, beat egg and egg yolks until creamy and thick. Add sugar and salt and continue to beat for a few minutes.

2. Place the yolk mixture over boiling water and cook until thick, stirring constantly. Remove from heat.

3. Add lemon juice and rind to yolk mixture and blend through. Let cool.

4. Beat egg whites stiff and fold into lemon mixture.

5. Whip cream, blend in powdered sugar, and fold into lemon filling.

6. Pour lemon mixture into refrigerator tray with graham cracker crust. Sprinkle remaining 1/3 cup crumbs over the top and refrigerate for at least three hours before serving or overnight.

7. When ready to serve, cut into squares.

Yield: 6 servings

Frozen Peach Dessert

24 macaroons

2 cups mashed fresh
  peaches (5 to 6
  peaches)

1 tablespoon fresh
  lemon juice

1 cup sugar

1/2 pint heavy cream

1. Dry macaroons at room temperature for several days and make crumbs in blender or with rolling pin. Spread half of the crumbs in a quart size shallow pan to make a bottom crust.

2. Drop peaches in boiling water and let stand until skins come off easily. Peel, cut up in small pieces and mash with a fork or chop in blender.

3. Sprinkle lemon juice on peaches and mix in sugar.

4. Whip cream stiff and fold into mashed peaches.

5. Pour peach mixture onto crumb crust. Sprinkle remaining crumbs over top and cover with foil. Freeze from 4 to 6 hours or until firm.

6. Remove from freezer half an hour before serving. Cut into squares and keep in refrigerator until ready to serve.

Yield: 6 to 8 servings

The recipe may be doubled and made in a spring form for more people.

Lemon-Blueberry Refrigerator Dessert

4 eggs

1 cup sugar

2 cups milk, scalded

1/8 teaspoon salt

2 tablespoons flour

juice of 1 large lemon, strained

1/2 pint heavy cream, whipped stiff

1 cup fresh blueberries, washed

1/2 cup water

1/4 cup sugar

10 ladyfingers

1. In top of double boiler, mix sugar, salt, and flour into beaten eggs. Very slowly pour in scalded milk.

2. Cook over low heat, stirring constantly until mixture thickens to soft custard. This takes about 10 minutes.

3. After custard is cool, stir in strained lemon juice.

4. Carefully line an 8 × 6-inch pan with waxed paper. Spread whipped cream over bottom and sides, saving about 5 tablespoons for the top.

5. Place pan in freezing compartment to allow cream to set.

6. Combine blueberries, water, and sugar and cook slowly for about 2 minutes. DO NOT BOIL. Drain off water completely.

7. Split lady fingers and place 10 halves on top of the set whipped cream in pan.

8. Sprinkle berries on top of lady fingers and then cover with lemon filling.

9. Top with remaining 10 lady finger halves and garnish with the 5 tablespoons whipped cream. Chill for about 2 hours in freezing compartment of refrigerator.

Yield: 4 to 6 servings

VIENNESE TORTE

1/2 pound vanilla wafers

1/3 cup ground walnuts

1/4 cup melted butter

1/2 cup soft butter

1 cup confectioners' sugar

2 eggs, separated

———

1 pint sugared raspberries or strawberries

1 cup heavy cream

1 tablespoon sifted confectioners' sugar

1. Make crumbs of vanilla wafers in blender or with rolling pin and mix with ground nuts. Add melted butter. Divide crumb mixture in half, using one half to line a buttered 9-inch spring form for the bottom crust. Set aside other half.

2. Cream soft butter, add powdered sugar, and blend thoroughly.

3. Add egg yolks, one at a time, to cream mixture, beating thoroughly.

4. Beat the egg whites until stiff and fold into above mixture.

5. Spread this mixture on layer of crumb-nut mixture.

6. Arrange sweetened berries over surface of cream mixture.

7. Whip cream, add sugar, and whip some more until cream holds its peaks. Cover berries with whipped cream.

8. Sprinkle remaining crumbs over top of whipped cream.

9. Refrigerate overnight.

Yield: 8 servings

Louisiana Rum Cream

5 egg yolks
3/4 cup sugar
1/4 cup rum
1/2 pint heavy cream
2 teaspoons sugar
1 dozen ladyfingers

1. Beat yolks thoroughly, add sugar and continue to beat.

2. Mix rum into egg yolks.

3. Beat cream until stiff. Add sugar and beat a little longer. Gradually fold whipped cream into yolk mixture.

4. Cut ladyfinger halves lengthwise and line a shallow serving dish.

5. Pour half the cream mixture over the ladyfingers, cover with ladyfingers, and pour remaining cream mixture over this, making 2 layers of ladyfingers and rum cream.

6. Refrigerate for several hours or better yet overnight.

Yield: about 6 servings.

Orange Blossom Bowl

12 ladyfingers

1 pint heavy cream

2 tablespoons honey

6 tablespoons frozen
    orange juice concen-
    trate, undiluted (1/2
    of six-ounce can)

1 orange, sectioned

1. Split ladyfingers and line bottom and sides of a glass serving dish.

2. Whip cream stiff. Fold in honey and undiluted orange juice.

3. Pour cream mixture into dish lined with ladyfingers. Chill in refrigerator for at least 4 hours or more.

4. When ready to serve, garnish with orange sections.

Yield: 6 servings

When you have an unexpected guest to dinner, try this delightful and easy-to-put-together dessert. Sponge or pound cake may be used in place of ladyfingers.

Strawberries Divine

1 cup unsalted butter

1 cup sugar

1/2 cup orange liqueur

1 cup ground walnuts

1 pint heavy cream

1 quart fresh
   strawberries

2 dozen ladyfingers

1. Allow butter to soften at room temperature and then cream it with sugar until light and fluffy.

2. Beat in orange liqueur and ground nuts.

3. Beat the cream thick and fold into butter mixture.

4. Wash, hull, and drain berries.

5. Line a 6-cup mold with waxed paper. Line with split ladyfingers, split side in. Sprinkle on some brandy and spoon in one-third of cream mixture. Put in layer of berries and cover with ladyfingers. Repeat until mold is filled.

6. Cover with waxed paper and refrigerate overnight.

7. To unmold, run knife around inside of mold and turn over on serving dish. Remove wax paper and refrigerate until serving time. Sauce may be used and additional strawberries to decorate the plate.

Yield: 8 servings

STRAWBERRY SAUCE

*1 quart fresh
    strawberries*

1/2 cup sugar

3 tablespoons brandy

1. Wash, hull and drain the berries.

2. Whip in blender. Stir in the sugar and brandy.

Yield: About 1½ cups

The only substitution I have found to be as delicious and pretty is fresh raspberries. The mold needs to be refrigerated overnight so that the butter will be firm; otherwise it will collapse when unmolded.

Strawberry Crunch Parfait

CRUNCH

3/4 cup quick oats,
  uncooked

1/4 cup flaked or
  shredded coconut

2 tablespoons firmly
  packed brown sugar

3 tablespoons melted
  butter or margarine

1. Combine the oats, coconut, brown sugar, and melted butter.

2. Spread above mixture over a shallow baking pan and bake in a preheated oven of 350° for 10 minutes.

3. Remove from oven and stir through. Allow to cool.

In England the strawberry leaf on the coronet of a nobleman symbolizes his rank! A marquis has four strawberry leaves on his golden coronet while an earl must be contented with a few leaves alternated with pearls. The travails of nobility! But let us consider the noble fruit itself.

PARFAIT FILLING

*2 cups fresh
  strawberries*

1/3 cup sugar

*2 quarts softened
  vanilla ice cream*

*commercial marsh-
  mallow topping*

1. Wash, hull, and slice strawberries. Sprinkle with sugar and refrigerate for 20 minutes.

2. After refrigeration, drain off any juice that has been formed.

3. In a 9-inch-square pan, spread one-third of the softened ice cream to make a layer. Then distribute half the drained berries evenly over the ice cream and sprinkle half of the crunch over the strawberry layer.

Repeat with layers of ice cream, strawberries, and crunch. Top with remaining ice cream, cover with waxed paper, and freeze overnight.

If there is any remaining crunch, refrigerate for later use.

4. When ready to serve, remove from refrigerator, cut in squares, and spoon marshmallow topping over each square. Then sprinkle with reserved crunch. Serve in parfait or tall stemmed glasses.

Yield: 12 servings

Pineapple Ice Box Cake

CRUST

1-1/2 cups graham
    cracker crumbs

1/3 cup confectioners'
    sugar

1/2 cup chopped nuts

1/2 cup melted butter

1. Mix crumbs, sugar, nuts and butter well. Set aside ¼ cup for garnish. Use the remainder to make crust in a 10 × 6 × 1½-inch pan.

FILLING

1/4 pound butter or
    margarine

3/4 cup confectioners'
    sugar

2 egg yolks, beaten

2 egg whites

1/8 teaspoon salt

1 one-pound can
    crushed pineapple

1/2 pint heavy cream

2 tablespoons
    confectioners' sugar

1. Cream butter and sugar.

2. Add beaten yolks to butter mixture.

3. Beat egg whites and salt until stiff. Fold into cream filling mixture. Then pour onto crust.

4. Drain pineapple, making certain that there is no juice left in the fruit.

5. Whip cream stiff and fold in sugar. Then mix pineapple into whipped cream.

6. Gently place pineapple mixture over cream filling and sprinkle with reserved graham cracker crumbs.

7. Refrigerate overnight.

Yield: 10 servings

Pineapple Mousse

1 small can frozen
  pineapple juice

juice of 1 lemon,
  strained

1/2 pint heavy cream

1 tablespoon
  confectioners' sugar

1 tablespoon grated
  coconut

1. Allow frozen pineapple juice to soften and mix in lemon juice.

2. Beat cream until thick. Add sugar and continue beating until stiff.

3. Carefully fold cream into juice mixture until evenly blended.

4. Pour mixture into a refrigerator tray and freeze until edges begin to harden.

5. Then turn mixture into a bowl and beat for several minutes. Return to tray and keep in freezer for about one hour or until almost firm.

6. While mousse is setting in freezer, toast coconut in a shallow pan in a 375°F. oven.

7. Serve mousse in sherbet glasses and sprinkle toasted coconut over top.

Yield: 4 servings

Peppermint Candy Fluff

CRUST

1-1/2 cups vanilla wafer
    crumbs

2 tablespoons sugar

1/4 cup butter, melted

1. Mix sugar and crumbs in bowl.

2. Melt butter and mix well with crumbs.

Spread half of crumbs over bottom of
6 × 8-inch baking dish.

FILLING

1 pint heavy cream

1/2 pound
    marshmallows
    (about 22)

1 cup peppermint
    pillows

1. Beat cream stiff. Cut marshmallows
into small pieces and mix with whipped
cream.

2. Crush candy and fold into marsh-
mallow-whipped cream.

3. Spread mixture over crumbs and top
with remaining half of crumb mixture.

4. Refrigerate overnight. When ready
to serve, cut into squares.

Yield: 8 servings

Cakes and Tortes

Contents

There is no such thing as a "born cook" who instinctively creates miracles in the kitchen. Expert cooks know that epicurean cakes and tortes are the result of simply paying attention to the basic rules of baking. If you are a novice, you need only pay attention as well, and you can become the proverbial "born cook."

And don't forget

- Read the entire recipe—ingredients and instructions—before beginning.
- If your ingredients are all at room temperature before you begin cooking, you will make a fluffier cake.
- Always preheat the oven (to the specified cooking temperature).
- Measurements should be level (unless otherwise specified).
- Measurements specified in a recipe must be exact.
- Sift flour before measuring.
- Where another flour is not specified, use all-purpose flour.
- Cake flour is finer than all-purpose flour and is used in many of these recipes. If you have none, you may sift all-purpose flour three times and then use slightly less than the recipe calls for.
- When directions say to add flour alternately, begin and finish with the flour. This makes a fluffier batter.
- After greasing cakepan, dust with flour and shake out excess before pouring in batter.
- For fruitcakes, line the baking pans with aluminum foil and then grease the foil.
- Shiny metal pans are preferable to glass pans. But if glass pans are used, set oven temperature 25 degrees lower than specified in the recipe.
- If you open the oven door before one-fourth of the baking time has elapsed, the cake will not rise properly nor brown evenly. You should not at any time during the baking open the door unnecessarily.

- Be certain cake is done. When minimum baking time is up, touch center of top surface lightly. No imprint should remain. A second test is to see if a toothpick inserted into the center comes out clean.
- After removing cakes from the oven, leave them in the pans to cool for about fifteen minutes, then circle the edges with a knife to loosen them.
- To remove the cakes from the pans, invert a cooling rack over the top of the cake. Then turn cake and rack upside down together and lift off the pan.
- Fruitcakes should be stored in airtight containers in a cool place for at least a week before they are served so that the flavors will blend.
- Glazes for tarts or cakes can be made from either apricot preserves or red currant jelly—boil them first and let cool before painting the top.
- If you frost the cake before it is cold, the icing will soften and run down the cake. Wait.

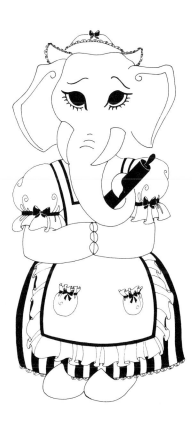

Bing Cherry Torte

8 egg yolks

1 cup plus 3 tablespoons confectioners' sugar

1-1/2 cups FRESH rye bread crumbs (about 4 slices)

3 tablespoons sweet sherry

1 cup ground walnuts

grated rind of 1 lemon

dash of cinnamon

8 egg whites beaten stiff enough to hold point

3 sixteen-ounce cans pitted black Bing cherries

——————

1 cup heavy cream

4 tablespoons granulated sugar

2 teaspoons vanilla

Preheat oven to 350°F.

1. Beat egg yolks and sugar until *very smooth.*

2. Cut crusts off bread and make crumbs in blender. Stir crumbs into egg mixture.

3. Add sherry and ground nuts to batter and blend well.

4. Stir in grated lemon rind and cinnamon.

5. Fold stiffly beaten egg whites into crumb mixture.

6. Drain cherries well. It is very important that there is no liquid whatsoever. Reserve half can of the well-drained cherries for a garnish.

7. Gently fold the 2-1/2 cans of drained cherries into the cake batter.

8. Butter and lightly flour a 10-inch spring form. Pour in batter and bake in a preheated oven for 30 to 45 minutes.

9. When cake is tested done with a toothpick, remove from oven and cool on a cake rack.

10. After cake is completely cool, beat cream stiff and add sugar and vanilla.

11. Remove cool cake to a plate and cover completely with whipped cream. Decorate top with a ring of black cherries.

Yield: 10 servings.

Buttermilk Chocolate Cake

2 ounces unsweetened chocolate

2 teaspoons baking soda

1 cup boiling water

1/4 pound butter or margarine

2 cups brown sugar

2 eggs, beaten

2 cups sifted cake flour

1/2 teaspoon salt

1/2 cup buttermilk

2 teaspoons vanilla

Preheat oven to 350 F.

1. Melt chocolate in a deep saucepan, stir in baking soda, and remove from heat. Add boiling water at once but DO NOT STIR. The mixture will bubble to top of saucepan. Cool.

2. While chocolate is cooling, cream butter and sugar. Add beaten eggs and blend thoroughly.

3. Measure and sift flour and salt. Add alternately with buttermilk and cooled chocolate mixture. Blend in vanilla.

4. Pour batter into greased 9 × 12-inch loaf pan. Bake 45 minutes or until tester comes out clean.

5. Dust with confectioners' sugar or frost with Seven Minute Icing.

SEVEN MINUTE ICING

2 egg whites

1 cup granulated sugar

3 tablespoons water

1/2 teaspoon cream of tartar

1/4 teaspoon salt

1 teaspoon vanilla

Put all ingredients except vanilla in a double boiler. Beat over hot water for about 5 minutes, or until frosting stands in peaks. Remove from heat. Add vanilla and beat for a few more minutes until thick enough to spread.

Blitz Torte

1/2 cup butter

1 cup sugar

4 eggs, separated

1/2 teaspoon vanilla

1-1/2 cup sifted flour

2 teaspoons baking
  powder

1/2 cup milk

———

4 egg whites

1/4 teaspoon cream of
  tartar

1 cup sugar

1/2 teaspoon vanilla

3 tablespoons sliced or
  chopped blanched
  almonds

1 tablespoon sugar

1/2 teaspoon cinnamon

Preheat oven to 350°F.

1. Cream shortening and sugar. Beat in egg yolks one at a time. Add vanilla.

2. Sift together flour and baking powder and add to creamed mixture alternately with milk.

3. Spread batter into 2 greased and floured 9-inch-round cake pans.

4. Beat 4 egg whites with cream of tartar until foamy. Add vanilla and 1 cup sugar a little at a time. Continue beating until egg whites are stiff. Spread over both unbaked batters.

5. Mix nuts, sugar, and cinnamon and sprinkle over both pans; bake for about 30 minutes.

6. When cakes are finished, remove from pans and cool on a rack.

7. Put the two layers together with a custard filling between, or with sweetened cut up fruit topped with sweetened whipped cream.

CUSTARD FILLING

2 tablespoons sugar

2 tablespoons cornstarch

1/4 teaspoon salt

1 cup milk

2 eggs, beaten

1 teaspoon vanilla

1. Mix sugar, cornstarch and salt in saucepan.

2. Slowly stir in milk. Cook and stir over medium heat until mixture thickens and boils. Cook several minutes longer.

3. Stir a little hot mixture into eggs. Return to hot mixture. Stirring constantly, bring just to boil.

4. Add vanilla and cool.

Yield: about 16 servings

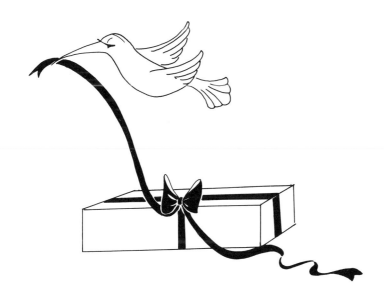

Chewy Chocolate Cake

8 ounces semisweet
  chocolate

1 tablespoon instant
  coffee

8 ounces sweet butter

1 cup sugar

8 eggs, separated

2 squares unsweetened
  baking chocolate

Preheat oven to 325°F.

1. Melt chocolate and instant coffee in top of double boiler.

2. Mix butter and sugar thoroughly and add melted chocolate-coffee mixture.

3. Add egg yolks, one at a time, continuing the beating between additions, at a very low speed. BEAT AT LOW SPEED FOR 25 MINUTES.

4. Then carefully fold in stiffly beaten egg whites until completely blended.

5. Butter only the bottom of a 9-inch spring form, not the sides. Pour in 3/4 of the mixture, saving the remainder for later.

6. Bake for about 35 minutes or until testing straw comes out clean. Then remove from oven and allow to cool. The cake will fall in the center.

7. When cake is completely cool, spread remaining batter over top and grate chocolate over it.

8. Cover with waxed paper and refrigerate until ready to serve. Allow at least several hours of chilling.

Yield: 12 servings

The trick to this cake is the long beating time. You can make this a day in advance. It is a rich and chewy torte and even richer when served with soft whipped cream. This recipe has been handed down through three generations. Wasn't I lucky to inherit it!

Cheese Torte

1 six-ounce package
  zwieback

3/4 cup sugar

1 teaspoon cinnamon

3 tablespoons melted
  butter or margarine

1-1/2 pounds pot cheese
  or dry cottage cheese

1 cup commercial sour
  cream

1 cup sugar

6 eggs, separated

grated rind of 2 lemons

2 tablespoons flour

1/4 teaspoon salt

Preheat oven to 325°F.

1. Make fine crumbs of zwieback in blender or with rolling pin. Mix together with sugar, cinnamon, and melted butter. Set aside 1/2 cup for topping.

2. Butter a 10-inch spring form well and spread crumb mixture over bottom and sides to make crust. Bake in preheated oven for 5 minutes. Cool.

3. In a bowl, beat cheese until smooth, add sour cream and sugar and beat until fluffy. Adding one egg yolk at a time, continue beating.

4. Stir in grated rind and flour.

5. Beat egg whites and salt until stiff and fold into batter. Then pour into zwieback-lined form and sprinkle top with remaining crumb mixture. Bake in preheated oven for 1 hour. When finished baking, turn off heat and let torte remain in oven with the door open for another hour or until cooled. Remove rim of spring form and chill well before serving.

Yield: about 10 servings

Russian Walnut Torte

12 eggs, separated

3-1/2 cups
   confectioners' sugar

1 teaspoon vanilla

3 tablespoons crushed
   oven dried ladyfingers

juice and rind of 1 lemon

1/4 teaspoon salt

1 pound walnuts,
   finely chopped

Preheat oven to 325°F.

1. Beat egg yolks and slowly beat in sugar until well blended. Stir in vanilla.

2. Stir in ladyfinger crumbs, lemon juice and rind.

3. Add salt to egg whites and beat until stiff. Very slowly begin to fold chopped nuts and egg whites into yolk mixture.

4. Pour batter into three 9-inch greased and floured cake pans. Bake in preheated oven for 40 to 50 minutes, until cake tests done. Remove from pan, cool on rack, and then refrigerate until cake is thoroughly chilled.

1/2 cup butter

3-1/2 cups (or 1 pound) confectioners' sugar

2 teaspoons vanilla

4 to 5 tablespoons cream

2 teaspoons instant coffee

3 tablespoons rum

1 four-ounce jar commercial apricot filling or apricot jam warmed and pureed

walnut halves for garnish

FROSTING

1. Whip butter and sugar until smooth. Stir in vanilla. Add enough cream to make spreading consistency.

2. Make paste of coffee with small amount of water and mix with rum.

3. Sprinkle rum-coffee mixture on each layer of cake. Spread apricot filling between layers, then frost cake and decorate with walnut halves.

Yield: 12-14 servings

Chocolate Mayonnaise Cake

1 cup sugar

1/2 teaspoon salt

1 teaspoon cinnamon

2 tablespoons grated
semisweet chocolate

1 cup mayonnaise

1 cup boiling water

1 teaspoon baking soda

1/2 cup chopped walnuts

1/2 cup chopped dates
or raisins

1-3/4 cups sifted all-
purpose flour

1 teaspoon vanilla

Preheat oven to 350°F.

1. Mix sugar, salt, cinnamon and chocolate in bowl.

2. Add mayonnaise and blend.

3. In separate bowl, pour boiling water and add soda. Allow water to fizz until action subsides.

4. Pour water-soda mixture over combined nuts and dates or raisins. Let stand several minutes.

5. Combine both mixtures and blend well.

6. Add sifted flour to above batter and blend thoroughly. Stir in vanilla.

7. Grease a 9-inch loaf pan and bake for about 40 minutes or until tested done.

8. Remove from oven and cool before removing from pan.

Yield: about 12 servings

An important trick is to allow date-nut mixture enough time to soak. A good topping for this cake is softened cream cheese flavored with grated orange rind.

Danish Applesauce Torte

2 cups lightly sweetened
applesauce

1/2 cup confectioners'
sugar

1-1/4 cups finely ground
blanched almonds

3 eggs, separated

1 cup heavy cream,
whipped (optional)

1 teaspoon vanilla

1 tablespoon
confectioners' sugar

Preheat oven to 350°F.

1. Spread applesauce in an 8 × 8-inch buttered baking dish.

2. Combine sugar and ground nuts. Beat in egg yolks one at a time until completely blended.

3. Gently fold in stiffly beaten egg whites and spread over applesauce.

4. Set the dish in a shallow pan of hot water and bake torte in preheated oven for about 15 minutes. The meringue should be set and lightly browned.

5. Serve warm, with whipped cream that has been flavored with vanilla and confectioners' sugar.

Yield: 6 servings

Devil's Food Potato Cake
(Kartoffel Torte)

1 cup butter or
  margarine

1-3/4 cups granulated
  sugar

4 eggs, separated

1 cup warm mashed
  potatoes (about
  2 medium)

2 cups all-purpose
  flour

2 teaspoons baking
  powder

2 teaspoons cinnamon

1 teaspoon nutmeg

1/4 teaspoon salt

1/2 cup light cream

1/2 cup grated baking
  chocolate

1/2 cup chopped walnuts

Preheat oven to 325 F.

1. Cream butter and sugar until light and fluffy.

2. Add beaten egg yolks. Stir in mashed potatoes and blend well.

3. Sift all dry ingredients. Add alternately to above mixture with cream, beginning and ending with flour mixture.

4. Fold grated chocolate and chopped nuts into batter.

5. Beat egg whites stiff and fold into batter.

6. Butter and lightly flour two 9-inch-round layer cake pans. Divide batter between two pans. Bake for about 25 minutes or until cake tester comes out clean. A 9 × 3-inch tube spring form pan may be used. In this form, bake for 1 hour and 25 minutes.

7. Remove from oven and cool in pan for 10 minutes.

8. Remove from pan, cool on rack and frost with butter cream, fudge frosting, or dust with sieved confectioners' sugar.

Yield: about 10 servings

FUDGE FROSTING

6 ounces semisweet
   chocolate

1/4 cup butter

1/2 cup sour cream

dash of salt

1 teaspoon vanilla

3 cups (approximately)
   confectioners' sugar

1. Melt chocolate and butter together in saucepan.

2. Blend in sour cream, salt and vanilla.

3. Cream in confectioners' sugar until of good spreading consistency.

Yield: 2-1/2 cups

French Coffee Cake

2 cups all-purpose
    flour

1-1/2 cups sugar

2 teaspoons baking
    powder

1/2 teaspoon salt

1/2 pound butter or
    margarine

2 eggs, slightly beaten

3/4 cup milk

1 teaspoon vanilla

2 teaspoons cinnamon

Preheat oven to 350°F.

1. In a bowl, sift together flour, sugar, baking powder, and salt.

2. Cut shortening into flour mixture with a pastry blender. Texture should be coarse.

3. Set aside 1 cup of above mixture to be used for topping.

4. Add eggs, milk, and vanilla to flour mixture and blend well.

5. Pour batter into a buttered 6 × 8-inch cake pan. Spread topping mixture over the cake.

7. Bake for about 25 minutes or until cake is tested done.

Yield: about 6 servings

Mock Cheese Torte

2 cups fine graham cracker crumbs

1/2 teaspoon cinnamon

1/4 cup finely chopped walnuts

1/4 pound melted butter

1 fifteen-ounce jar unsweetened apple sauce

1 cup condensed milk

4 eggs, separated

1 lemon—strained juice and grated rind

1 teaspoon salt added to egg whites before beating

Preheat oven to 350°F.

1. Combine crumbs, cinnamon, nuts and butter. Grease bottom and sides of a 9-inch spring form pan and press crumbs on bottom and sides to form crust. Save 1/2 cup for topping.

2. In a bowl, stir applesauce, condensed milk, egg yolks, lemon juice and grated rind together. Blend thoroughly.

3. Carefully fold in beaten egg whites and salt.

4. Pour batter into pan and sprinkle top with remaining graham cracker crumb mixture. Bake for 1 hour.

5. After cake is removed from oven, cool and then refrigerate for several hours or overnight before serving.

Yield: 8-10 servings

Glazed Orange Cake

1 cup butter

2-1/2 cups sugar

6 large eggs

3 cups all-purpose
    flour

1/2 teaspoon salt

1/4 teaspoon baking soda

1 cup sour cream

1 teaspoon grated
    orange rind

1 teaspoon vanilla

Preheat oven to 350°F.

1. Beat butter until light and fluffy. Add sugar and continue to beat until well blended.

2. Add eggs one at a time, beating after each addition.

3. Sift together flour, salt, and soda.

4. Alternately, add flour and sour cream to butter mixture, beginning and ending with dry ingredients.

5. Stir in orange rind and vanilla. Batter should be well blended.

6. Grease and lightly flour a 10-inch tube pan. Spoon batter into pan, distributing evenly.

7. Bake in preheated oven for 1 hour and 20 minutes, or until tested done. Because ovens vary, check after an hour of baking. Don't allow cake to be overbaked and dry.

8. Pour hot glaze over entire cake and let rest for one hour before removing from pan. If there is extra glaze, serve with cake.

ORANGE GLAZE

1 cup orange juice

1 tablespoon lemon juice

3/4 cup granulated sugar

1/4 cup butter

1. Combine juices, sugar, and butter in saucepan. Bring to a boil, lower heat, and simmer for 10 minutes.

2. For faster absorption, poke holes in cake with cake tester or toothpick before pouring over glaze.

Yield: about 12-14 servings

WHITE HOUSE CARROT CAKE

2 cups all-purpose flour

2 teaspoons baking soda

1 teaspoon salt

1 teaspoon cinnamon

2 cups sugar

1-1/2 cups vegetable oil

4 eggs

3 cups grated raw carrots

1 teaspoon vanilla

1 cup chopped walnuts

Preheat oven to 350°F.

1. Sift dry ingredients into a large mixing bowl.

2. Add oil and blend well.

3. Beat eggs slightly and stir into above mixture.

4. Fold in grated carrots.

5. Add vanilla and nuts and mix well. Batter should be smooth and well blended.

6. Pour into a well greased 9-inch tube pan and bake for about 1-1/2 hours or until tested done.

7. Remove cake from oven and glaze while still hot.

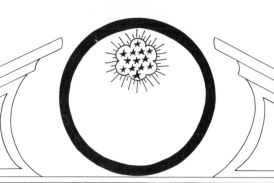

BUTTERMILK GLAZE

1/2 cup buttermilk

1 cup sugar

1/2 teaspoon
baking soda

1 tablespoon white
corn syrup

1. Blend all ingredients well and pour uncooked glaze on top of hot cake in pan. Let stand one hour before removing from pan, in order to let glaze become firm and cake cool.

2. To remove cake from pan, run a spatula around the sides of the tube and lift it out. Use two broad spatulas between cake and bottom of pan to lift cake to a serving plate.

Oatmeal Cake

1 cup uncooked oats

1-1/3 cups boiling water

1 cup shortening

1 cup granulated sugar

1 cup brown sugar

2 eggs, beaten

1-1/3 cups all-purpose flour

1 teaspoon baking soda

1 teaspoon baking powder

1 teaspoon cinnamon

1/2 teaspoon salt

1 teaspoon vanilla

Preheat oven to 325°F.

1. Soak oats in boiling water for 20 minutes.

2. While soaking oats, cream sugars and shortening.

3. Add eggs one at a time, beating well.

4. Add oats to creamed mixture.

5. Sift dry ingredients together and add to creamed mixture.

6. Blend in vanilla.

7. Pour batter into a 9 × 12-inch greased and lightly floured pan.

8. Bake in preheated oven for about 35 minutes or until tested done. Remove from oven and immediately spread with topping.

TOPPING

1 cup brown sugar

4 tablespoons butter or margarine

1 cup flaked coconut

1/2 cup chopped nuts

1/3 cup light cream

1. Cream sugar and shortening.

2. Add coconut and nuts and blend well.

3. Moisten coconut mixture with cream and spread over top of cake. Return to oven and broil for a few minutes until topping solidifies and oozes over top of cake.

Yield: about 12 servings

Sour Cream Kuchen

1/2 cup butter or
    margarine

1 cup granulated sugar

2 eggs

2 cups all-purpose flour

1 teaspoon baking
    powder

1 teaspoon baking
    soda

1/2 teaspoon salt

1 cup sour cream

1 teaspoon vanilla

Preheat oven to 325°F.

1. Cream butter and sugar until batter is light yellow.

2. Add eggs one at a time, beating well after each addition.

3. Sift dry ingredients together and add to batter alternately with sour cream, beginning and ending with dry ingredients.

4. Blend in vanilla.

TOPPING AND FILLING

1/3 cup light brown sugar

1/4 cup granulated sugar

1 teaspoon cinnamon

1/4 cup finely chopped
    pecans or walnuts

1. In a separate bowl combine all ingredients.

2. Pour half the batter into a well greased 8 × 12-inch cake pan and sprinkle half of nut filling over the top.

3. Then pour remaining cake batter over filling and top entire cake with remainder of nut filling.

4. Bake for about 40 minutes or until cake tester comes out dry.

Yield: 8 to 10 servings

Sachertorte

6 ounces semisweet
  chocolate

3/4 cup butter, softened

3/4 cup granulated sugar

8 egg yolks

10 egg whites

pinch of salt

1 cup cake flour, sifted

Preheat oven to 350°F.

1. Melt chocolate in top of a double boiler.

2. Blend sugar into softened butter and stir in melted chocolate.

3. Add yolks, one at a time, to chocolate mixture.

4. Beat egg whites with salt until stiff peaks form. Carefully fold in flour and gently stir into chocolate mixture.

5. Butter and flour two 8-inch cake tins. Divide batter between pans and bake slowly in preheated oven until testing straw comes out clean, about 25 minutes.

6. Remove pans from oven, cool 5 minutes and then turn over on rack to cool. When completely cool, remove from tins and prepare glaze.

GLAZE

4 ounces unsweetened chocolate

1 cup confectioners' sugar

2 tablespoons HOT water

1 egg, well beaten

4 tablespoons butter

1 teaspoon vanilla

———

1/4 cup apricot jam, warmed and sieved

1 cup heavy cream, whipped

1. Melt chocolate in top of double boiler over boiling water.

2. Remove pan from water and stir in sugar. Then blend in hot water.

3. Stir a small amount of chocolate mixture into beaten egg and then return egg to chocolate and beat well.

4. Add small amounts of butter at a time to mixture, beating after each addition.

5. Stir in vanilla.

6. When cake layers are completely cool, spread jam on one layer, cover with second layer and pour glaze evenly over entire cake. Smooth with a spatula.

7. After glaze stops dripping, transfer to a clean plate, refrigerate until glaze hardens.

8. Serve whipped cream in a separate bowl.

Sachertorte is a Viennese specialty and was originated at the Sacher Hotel in Vienna. The story goes that Prince Metternich asked Mr. Sacher to make a more masculine gateau. The rich creamy creations were for women, he claimed.

Surprise Cake

3/4 cup butter

2 cups sugar

3 eggs

3 cups sifted cake flour

3 teaspoons baking
    powder

1/4 teaspoon salt

1 cup milk

1 tablespoon vanilla

2-1/2 cups heavy cream,
    whipped

6 tablespoons
    confectioners' sugar

1 tablespoon vanilla

1/4 cup chopped walnuts

Preheat oven to 375°F.

1. Cream butter and sugar until light and fluffy. Add eggs one at a time, beating after each addition.

2. Sift flour again along with baking powder and salt.

3. Add flour alternately to batter with milk. Stir in vanilla.

4. Butter and lightly flour a 9-inch spring form. Pour in batter and bake for about one hour or until a testing pin comes out clean.

5. Cool 10 minutes in pan and unmold on cake rack. When completely cool, turn cake over and cut off a one-inch layer of bottom of cake and carefully set aside. Then scoop out inside of cake, leaving a shell about one inch thick. Tear the soft pieces of cake into bite size and place in large bowl.

6. Whip cream; when cream begins to thicken, sprinkle in sugar and continue to beat until stiff. Add vanilla. Mix pieces of cake with sweetened whipped cream.

7. Fold in nuts and turn entire mixture back into cake shell. Replace bottom slice and stand cake upright. Refrigerate until ready to serve. Then ice with Chocolate Icing.

CHOCOLATE ICING

4 ounces semisweet chocolate

1/4 cup water

1/2 cup sugar

3 scant tablespoons water

2 teaspoons butter

2 tablespoons heavy cream

1. Melt chocolate in water until mixture is smooth.

2. In another saucepan, cook sugar and water for several minutes to make a syrup. Add chocolate to syrup, stirring until it boils.

3. Add butter and cream and continue to cook until thick. Stir, remove from heat. As soon as it cools, ice cake.

Yield: makes 8 servings

My mother created this recipe. She named it Surprise Cake. The surprise, of course, is the luscious whipped cream filling under a glaze of chocolate.

Swiss Banana Cake

1-1/2 cups sugar

1/2 cup butter or margarine

3 eggs, separated

1 cup mashed bananas (2 large)

1/4 cup buttermilk

3/4 cup chopped walnuts

2 cups all-purpose flour

1 teaspoon baking powder

1/2 teaspoon baking soda

1/2 teaspoon salt

1 teaspoon vanilla

Preheat oven to 350°F.

1. Gradually add sugar to butter and cream thoroughly.

2. Add one egg yolk at a time and blend in. Then add mashed bananas, buttermilk, and nuts.

3. Sift dry ingredients and add to above mixture.

4. Beat egg whites stiff. Fold into batter. Add vanilla.

5. Pour batter into two 9-inch greased cake tins and bake for 35-40 minutes or until tested done.

6. Remove from oven and cool. Frost with Mocha Frosting.

MOCHA FROSTING

1/4 pound butter

2 cups confectioners' sugar

6 tablespoons cocoa

1/4 teaspoon salt

4-6 tablespoons strong cold coffee

1 teaspoon vanilla

1. Cream butter and add sugar, cocoa and salt. Continue to beat until there is a smooth shiny look.

2. Add coffee and vanilla and blend thoroughly.

Viennese Gugelhupf

1/2 pound butter

1-1/2 cups sugar

4 whole eggs

3 cups cake flour

3 teaspoons baking powder

1/4 teaspoon salt

juice of 1 lemon

grated rind of 1 lemon

1 tablespoon vanilla

3/4 cup milk

confectioners' sugar

Preheat oven to 350°F.

1. Cream butter. Slowly add sugar, continuing to beat until fluffy.

2. Add eggs one at a time, beating after each addition until lemon color.

3. Measure flour and sift together with baking powder and salt.

4. Stir juice, rind, and vanilla into butter mixture.

5. Add flour and milk alternately, beginning and ending with dry ingredients. Blend well.

6. Butter and flour a bundt pan and spoon in batter.

7. Bake in preheated oven for one hour until it is light brown and tested done with cake tester.

8. Remove from oven and let it rest for 15 minutes before removing it from pan.

9. Turn out on a rack. When it is completely cool, dust with sifted confectioners' sugar.

Turkish Honey Cake

Preheat oven to 325°F.

1-1/2 cups zwieback crumbs, (about 2 dozen zwieback)

1-1/2 cups finely chopped walnuts

1-1/2 teaspoons baking powder

1/4 teaspoon salt

3/4 teaspoon cinnamon

5 eggs, separated

3/4 cup sugar

1 teaspoon vanilla extract

1. Grease a 9 × 9 × 2-inch pan. Mix crumbs and chopped walnuts in a large bowl.

2. Stir baking powder, salt, and cinnamon into crumb mixture.

3. In a smaller bowl, beat egg yolks until thick and light in color; then gradually beat in sugar. Blend in vanilla.

4. Work egg mixture into crumb mixture. A wooden spoon makes blending easier to accomplish since both mixtures are thick.

5. Beat egg whites until stiff and fold in. Turn batter into greased pan and bake for about 30 minutes. Remove from oven and cool for about 10 minutes. While cake is baking, prepare syrup.

Like most Middle Eastern desserts, Honey Cake is very sweet and should be served in very small portions.

SYRUP

Yield: 6-8 servings

2 cups water

1-1/2 cups sugar

2/3 cup honey

2 tablespoons light rum

1/2 cup heavy cream, whipped

1. In a medium sized saucepan, combine water, sugar, and honey. Bring to a boil, stirring occasionally. Then lower heat and simmer for 25 minutes.

2. Remove from heat and stir in rum.

3. Slowly pour syrup over cake in an even stream. Cover and let stand at room temperature for 6 hours. Serve with unsweetened whipped cream.

Tipsy Parson Cake

5 eggs, separated

juice and grated rind of
1 medium lemon

1-1/4 cups sifted
confectioners' sugar

1 cup cake flour

1/4 teaspoon salt

Preheat oven to 300°F.

1. Beat yolks with lemon juice and rind until light yellow.

2. Beat egg whites until soft peaks form. Gradually beat in sifted confectioners' sugar until stiff. Gently fold into yolk mixture.

3. Sift and measure flour and salt. Mix in 1/4 cup flour at a time to yolk mixture, rotating bowl as you do this.

4. Pour batter into an ungreased 9-inch-round spring form pan. Bake for about 45 minutes to an hour or until cake tester inserted in center comes out clean.

5. Remove cake from oven, cool for 5 minutes, and invert over a wire rack for 1 hour. When cake is cool, carefully loosen sides with a spatula and remove from pan.

SOFT CUSTARD

2 cups milk

4 egg yolks

1/2 cup sugar

dash of salt

2 tablespoons all-purpose
flour

1/2 teaspoon vanilla

1. Scald milk and cool to lukewarm.

2. In a bowl, beat egg yolks, gradually adding sugar, until light. Stir in salt and flour.

3. Slowly pour lukewarm milk into egg mixture, stirring constantly. When smoothly blended, cook in top of a double boiler over low heat. Continue to stir while thickening. Flavor with vanilla.

TO ASSEMBLE CAKE

1 cup brandy

1/2 pint heavy cream

*1 tablespoon sifted
    confectioners'
    sugar*

1. Cut cake into two layers. Place one layer in a large shallow glass bowl and sprinkle with 1/2 cup brandy.

2. Cover with half the custard, place second layer on top. Repeat procedure with other half cup brandy and remaining custard.

3. Whip cream, blend in sugar and cover top and sides of cake with the whipped cream. Refrigerate until ready to serve.

Yield: about 8 to 10 servings

Sicilian Cassata

1 nine-inch sponge cake

1-1/2 pounds ricotta or small curd creamed cottage cheese

3 tablespoons crème de cacao

3 tablespoons sugar

pinch of salt

1 teaspoon vanilla

2 tablespoons candied orange peel, chopped

2 ounces semisweet chocolate, grated

1. Cut cake into 3 layers.

2. Combine drained ricotta with crème de cacao, sugar, and salt and beat well. Mix in other ingredients.

3. Spread ricotta filling over layer of cake, cover with second layer, and spread filling over second layer. Top with third layer and chill. Then frost with Butter Cream Frosting.

BUTTER CREAM FROSTING

2 tablespoons sugar

1-1/2 tablespoons flour

1/4 cup cold milk

1/2 cup warm milk

1/4 cup butter

*1-1/2 cups sifted
    confectioners' sugar*

chopped nuts (optional)

1. Mix sugar, flour, and cold milk to form a paste. Stir in warm milk and cook over low heat until mixture thickens, stirring constantly. Cover and continue cooking over boiling water for another 5 minutes. Cover and cool.

2. Cream butter and sugar until smooth. Add cooled cream mixture. Spread sides and top of Cassata.

Yield: 12 servings

Cassata is served at Italian celebrations. If you prefer a chocolate butter cream frosting, add 2 ounces unsweetened melted chocolate with a tablespoon of grated orange rind to the frosting.

Cookies and Small Cakes

Contents

Cookies are a very versatile sweetmeat. For tea parties, buffets, or holidays and special occasions, attractively arranged, assorted cookies make an easy-to-serve dessert.

A plate of cookies can be introduced by itself, or combined with fruits, ice creams and dessert sauces. Most cookies can be prepared in advance and frozen to be used as the occasion demands. They can be rich or made of health foods for a more nutritious nibble.

The satisfaction of bringing neat, uniform cookies from the oven is a chef's reward. Perfect cookies should be evenly browned, crunchy and either crip or soft, depending on type.

And don't forget

• Dropped cookies are made by dropping spoonfuls of dough one inch apart on a buttered cookie sheet and flattening them with a fork dipped in cold water.

• Bar cookies are made by spreading the mixture on a buttered cookie sheet, baking and then cutting into squares.

• Drop cookie batter can be used for bar cookies, or vice versa, by increasing/decreasing the amount of liquid used.

• Refrigerator cookies are made from a cookie mixture firm enough to roll and form into sausage-like shapes, which are refrigerated. When thoroughly chilled and stiff (thirty minutes to an hour), they are sliced and baked. The dough can be refrigerated overnight if desired. Decorative indentations may be made on the cookies after they are cut with the tines of a fork.

• Always cover any butter cookie dough that is chilling in the refrigerator. This prevents dough from absorbing other food flavors and drying out.

• Filled cookies are made by putting together two already-baked cookies with jelly or tart filling in between.

• To make vanilla sugar, cut one vanilla bean apart, scrape out the inside and add it to one cup of sifted confectioners' sugar. Mix well, sift twice and store in a covered jar at least 24 hours.

• Cool large cookies for several minutes before removing them from the cookie sheet, unless otherwise directed. Just-baked cookies are tender and need time to become a bit firm.

• Most cookies are baked in a moderate oven (375°F.)

• Crisp cookies should be stored in a container with a loosely fitting lid to prevent softening.

• Soft cookies, on the other hand, should be kept in containers with tightly fitting lids and a piece of apple, orange or bread inside to keep them soft and moist.

Apricot Bars

1 cup dried apricots

1 cup water

1/2 cup soft butter or margarine

1/4 cup granulated sugar

2/3 cup all-purpose flour

———

2 eggs

1 cup light brown sugar

1/3 cup all-purpose flour

1/2 teaspoon baking powder

1/4 teaspoon salt

1/2 teaspoon vanilla

1/2 cup chopped nuts

Preheat oven to 350°F.

1. Rinse apricots, cover with water, and stew for 10 minutes. Drain, cool, and chop.

2. Cream butter, sugar, and flour. Then spread on a greased 8 × 8 × 2-inch pan.

3. Bake 15 or 20 minutes or until top is lightly browned.

4. While crust is baking, beat eggs and add the brown sugar.

5. To egg and sugar mixture, add flour, baking powder, and salt. Mix well.

6. Then add vanilla, nuts, and finally the chopped apricots. Blend thoroughly.

7. Remove crust from oven and spread entire filling over baked layer. Return to oven and bake for about another 30 minutes.

8. Remove from oven and cool in pan. Then cut into bars. Roll each bar in sugar.

Yield: 32 bars

Prepare filling while the first layer is baking so that it can be spread as soon as the crust is removed from the oven the first time. Then pop the pan back into the oven, and within half an hour you are ready for a special treat. These bars are delicious served with whipped cream.

Apricot Strudel

DOUGH

1/2 pound butter

1 eight-ounce package commercial sour cream (1 cup)

2 cups all-purpose flour

STRUDEL FILLING

1 twelve-ounce can prepared apricot filling

1/2 pound chopped walnuts

1 cup grated coconut

1 cup raisins (preferably light) or currants

granulated sugar

1. THE DAY BEFORE: Allow butter to soften at room temperature and mix with sour cream. Mix in flour until thoroughly blended. Dough will be sticky. Divide it in three balls, wrap each in waxed paper, and refrigerate dough overnight.

Preheat oven to 425°F.

1. The following day, work with one ball of dough at a time. Roll dough out on waxed paper in a rectangular shape. Because the dough gets sticky as it softens, it is important to generously sprinkle flour on rolling pin and dough as you work.

2. Spread with apricot filling within half inch of edges. Then sprinkle with chopped nuts, coconut, and raisins.

3. Roll up jelly roll fashion and tuck in sides. Place seam side down on shallow ungreased sheet. Repeat with remaining dough.

4. Sprinkle top with sugar and bake for about 15 minutes. Then reduce heat to 350°F. and bake strudel for 30 more minutes or until delicately brown.

5. Remove strudel from oven and while still hot, slice in diagonal bars. Cool on a rack.

Yield: 4-5 dozen

These can be frozen after baking and warmed in the oven for 10-15 minutes when you are ready to serve it.

Brandy Balls

1 twelve-ounce box
    vanilla wafers

1 cup finely chopped
    walnuts

1/4 cup brandy

1/4 cup rum

1/2 cup honey

sifted confectioners'
    sugar

1. Crush wafers into fine crumbs and combine with nuts.

2. Blend brandy and rum into crumb-nut mixture.

3. Thoroughly blend in honey.

4. Form into one-inch balls by rolling in palms of hands. Then roll each ball around in sifted confectioners' sugar.

To store brandy balls, wrap each one in waxed paper and place in tightly covered container.

Yield: about 60 balls

Cheese Squares with Jam (Topfenteig)

1 three-ounce package cream cheese

1/4 pound butter or margarine

1 cup cake flour

Preheat oven to 375°F.

1. Allow cream cheese and butter to reach room temperature. Then cream together until completely blended.

2. Mix cake flour into cheese mixture and stir well.

3. Form into ball and chill in refrigerator for 1 to 2 hours.

4. While dough is chilling, prepare filling.

FILLING

1 cup strawberry jam

1/4 cup ground walnuts

2 tablespoons graham cracker crumbs

1/4 cup confectioners' sugar

1. Blend together jam, nuts, and crumbs.

2. When dough is thoroughly chilled, remove it from refrigerator and roll it out on a slightly floured board or towel to about 1/4-inch thick.

3. Cut dough into 2-inch squares. Fill each square with about 1 teaspoon of filling. Then pinch all the edges together.

4. Bake on ungreased cookie sheet for about 12 to 15 minutes until lightly browned.

5. When cookies are finished baking, remove them from oven and allow to cool. Then sprinkle squares with confectioners' sugar.

Yield: about 2-1/2 dozen.

These can be prepared up to the baking step and kept refrigerated to be baked just before serving.

Bishop's Brot

6 eggs, separated

1 cup sugar

1/4 cup white raisins

2 ounces semisweet
chocolate, grated

2 tablespoons slivered
blanched almonds

1 tablespoon grated
lemon peel

1 tablespoon chopped
candied orange peel

1/2 teaspoon vanilla

1-1/4 cups all-purpose
flour

Preheat oven to 350°F.

1. Beat egg yolks and sugar until lemon color and smooth.

2. Combine raisins, grated chocolate, slivered almonds, grated lemon peel, and chopped candied peel and set aside.

3. Beat egg whites stiff, stir in vanilla, and fold into egg yolks.

4. Sift flour three times and carefully fold into egg mixture until it is evenly distributed.

5. Butter and flour a 9 × 13-inch pan. Pour half the batter in pan and spread evenly.

6. Sprinkle chocolate mixture over batter and cover with remaining batter.

7. Bake about 45 minutes, until tested done with cake tester.

8. Remove and cut into bars.

Yield: about 3-1/2 dozen pieces

Cherry Winks

3/4 cup shortening

1 cup sugar

2 eggs, slightly beaten

2 tablespoons milk

1 teaspoon vanilla

2-1/4 cups all-purpose
    flour

1 teaspoon baking
    powder

1/2 teaspoon baking soda

1/2 teaspoon salt

1 cup chopped walnuts

1/2 cup chopped dates

1/3 cup maraschino
    cherries, drained well
    and chopped

additional cherries for
    decoration

4 cups corn flakes,
    crushed

Preheat oven to 375°F.

1. Cream shortening and sugar thoroughly.

2. Add eggs, milk, and vanilla to above mixture and blend.

3. Sift the dry ingredients and add to blended mixture.

4. Mix nuts, dates, and cherries into mixture.

5. Drop rounded teaspoonfuls of batter into crushed flakes. Toss lightly so that they are completely covered with the flakes and form into balls.

6. Put cookies onto greased cookie sheet and top each with 1/4 of a maraschino cherry. Bake for 12-15 minutes.

Yield: about 9 dozen cookies

Chocolate Dream Bars

1 cup all-purpose flour

1/2 cup brown sugar

1/2 cup butter

———

1 cup brown sugar

2 tablespoons flour

1/2 teaspoon baking
    powder

1/4 teaspoon salt

1 twelve-ounce package
    of semisweet
    chocolate chips

1 teaspoon vanilla

2 eggs, slightly beaten

Preheat oven to 300°F.

1. Mix flour and sugar together.

2. With a pastry blender, cut butter into flour mixture until pieces are the size of peas.

3. Pat into a buttered 8 × 16-inch cookie sheet. Bake for about 20 minutes until slightly brown. While this is baking prepare the following:

4. Mix together sugar, flour, baking powder, salt, and chocolate chips.

5. Add the vanilla to the beaten eggs and blend into the brown sugar mixture.

6. When the first crust is slightly browned, remove it from oven and carefully spread chocolate chip mixture over entire baked mixture. Return it to oven and bake again at 300 degrees for about 15 to 20 minutes or until brown.

7. Remove from oven, cool, and cut into small squares.

Yield: 4½ dozen

Chocolate Pixies

1/2 cup butter or
   margarine

4 squares unsweetened
   chocolate

2 cups sugar

4 eggs

2 teaspoons vanilla

2 cups all-purpose flour

2 teaspoons baking
   powder

1/2 teaspoon salt

1/2 cup chopped walnuts

sifted confectioners'
   sugar

Preheat oven to 350°F.

1. Melt butter and chocolate in top of double boiler or in saucepan over low heat. Remove from heat and cool.

2. Blend sugar and eggs, adding one egg at a time, and beat well. Stir in vanilla.

3. Sift flour, baking powder, and salt and add to egg mixture.

4. Mix in melted chocolate and butter.

5. Add nuts to batter and stir well. Chill for at least 15 minutes.

6. Shape into balls, using about one tablespoon of dough for each. Roll in confectioners' sugar and place on a greased baking sheet.

7. Bake for 12-15 minutes.

Yield: about 4-1/2 dozen pixies

Cinnamon Squares

2 cups all-purpose flour

2 teaspoons cinnamon

1/4 teaspoons nutmeg

1 cup light brown sugar

1/2 pound butter or
   margarine

1 egg, separated

1/2 cup chopped walnuts

Preheat oven to 350°F.

1. Measure and mix flour, cinnamon, and nutmeg. Then mix in brown sugar.

2. Cut shortening in as for a pie crust until texture is like coarse crumbs.

3. Blend in beaten egg yolk.

4. Distribute dough over an ungreased 15 × 10-inch jelly roll pan and press down firmly with your hands.

5. Beat egg white slightly until frothy and brush over the surface.

6. Sprinkle nuts over top.

7. Bake for about 30 minutes or until edges begin to look brown.

8. Cool and cut in squares.

Yield: about 4 dozen

Coconut Crisps

1/2 cup butter or margarine

1/2 cup light brown sugar

1/2 cup granulated sugar

1 egg, slightly beaten

1 teaspoon vanilla

1-1/4 cups sifted all-purpose flour

1/2 teaspoon baking powder

1/2 teaspoon baking soda

1/2 teaspoon salt

1-1/2 cups shredded coconut

2 cups corn flakes

walnut halves

Preheat oven to 350°F.

1. Cream butter, sugars, egg, and vanilla until light and fluffy.

2. Stir in sifted dry ingredients until mixture is well blended.

3. Stir coconut and corn flakes into above mixture. Chill slightly for easy handling.

4. Shape into small balls about 3/4-inch in diameter. Place on ungreased baking sheet about 2-1/2 inches apart.

5. Lightly press a walnut half in center of each cookie.

6. Bake 12 to 15 minutes until lightly browned.

Yield: about 4 dozen crisps

Deluxe Lemon Bars

2 cups all-purpose flour

1/2 cup confectioners' sugar

1 cup butter or margarine

4 eggs

2 cups granulated sugar

1/2 teaspoon grated lemon rind

1/4 cup lemon juice

1/4 cup flour

1/2 teaspoon baking powder

confectioners' sugar

Preheat oven to 350°F.

1. Sift flour and sugar and cut in shortening so that texture appears like coarse crumbs.

2. Press into a 13 × 9 × 2-inch baking pan. Bake for 20 to 25 minutes or until lightly browned.

3. Beat together eggs, sugar, lemon rind, and juice.

4. Mix flour and baking powder together and stir into egg mixture.

5. Pour over baked crust.

6. Then return cookies to oven and bake 25 minutes longer.

7. When removed from oven, sprinkle with additional sifted confectioners' sugar.

8. Cool and then cut into bars.

Yield: about 4 dozen

Date-Nut Sweets, Unbaked

1 cup pitted dates,
    chopped

1/2 cup pecans, chopped

1/2 cup walnuts,
    chopped

grated rind of
    one medium orange

1 tablespoon orange
    juice

3 tablespoons
    confectioners' sugar

1 ounce unsweetened
    chocolate

2 tablespoons blanched
    almond pieces

1. Combine dates and nuts and stir in orange rind and juice.

2. Sprinkle confectioners' sugar on a board and roll out mixture about 1/4-inch thick. Cut in diamond shapes.

3. Melt chocolate over hot water and spread thinly over cookies.

4. Decorate each cookie with an almond sliver.

Yield: about 3 dozen

1 cup butter

2 cups sugar

juice and grated rind of
half lemon

6 large eggs

9-1/2 cups cake flour

5 tablespoons baking
powder

1/4 cup brandy

2 tablespoons milk

sesame seeds

Preheat oven to 375°F.

1. Cream butter and sugar until light and fluffy.

2. Stir juice and rind into butter mixture. Add eggs one at a time, beating after each addition.

3. Add half the flour and baking powder to batter. Then continue to slowly add remaining flour until the dough is stiff.

4. Blend in brandy and knead dough until it is smooth. Divide dough into quarters and roll out a quarter at a time.

5. Cut dough into thin strips and twist each strip into a circle.

6. Place circles on greased cookie sheet and brush tops with milk. Press sesame seeds into top of each.

7. Bake for about 12 to 15 minutes or until light brown.

Yield: about 9 dozen

This dry cookie is enjoyed with a cup of Greek or Turkish coffee. It is a specialty at Eastertime, and when we were in Athens, we noticed they were sold in the bakeries. The recipe may be made with additional butter for a richer cookie.

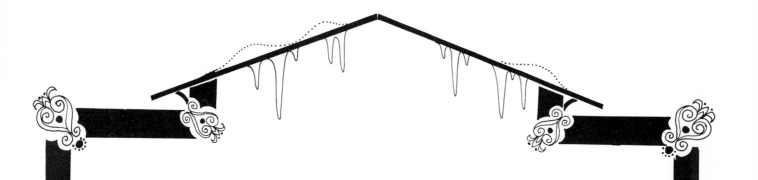

NORWEGIAN COOKIES

1 cup butter

1/2 cup sugar

1 teaspoon almond
extract

4 hard-cooked egg
yolks, sieved

2-1/2 cups all-purpose
flour

colored sugar

Preheat oven to 400°F.

1. Cream butter and sugar until fluffy.

2. Stir in sieved egg yolks and extract.

3. Sift and measure flour and blend into creamed mixture.

4. Chill dough for several hours or overnight.

5. Roll out and cut in shapes. Decorate with colored sugar and bake on ungreased cookie sheet for about 6 minutes.

Yield: about 5 dozen

Lemon Butter Cookies

2-1/4 cups all-purpose flour

1/2 teaspoon salt

1/4 teaspoon baking soda

1 cup butter

1/2 cup granulated sugar

1/2 cup light brown sugar, firmly packed

1 egg, beaten

1 tablespoon lemon juice

1 teaspoon grated lemon rind

Preheat oven to 375°F.

1. Sift together flour, salt, and soda.

2. Cream butter, add sugars, and mix thoroughly.

3. Beat in eggs, juice, and rind.

4. Stir in dry ingredients until they are completely blended.

5. Form into shapes or balls.

6. Bake on ungreased cookie sheet for 8 minutes.

Yield: 2 dozen

Mandel Brot

1 cup butter or
    margarine

1-1/2 cups sugar

4 eggs

4 cups all-purpose flour

1 teaspoon baking
    powder

1 teaspoon vanilla

1 cup nuts, chopped

2 teaspoons sugar

1 teaspoon cinnamon

Preheat oven to 350°F.

1. Cream butter and sugar. Add eggs one at a time, stirring after each addition.

2. Stir in flour and baking powder. Blend in vanilla.

3. Mix in nuts until thoroughly blended.

4. Mix sugar and cinnamon and set aside.

5. Divide dough to form 2-inch loaves about 16 inches long. Recipe should make about 9 loaves.

6. Bake in preheated oven for about 45 minutes until light brown.

7. Remove loaves from oven and slice them while hot into half-inch pieces. Slices are sprinkled with cinnamon-sugar and returned to oven to brown.

Yield: about 7 dozen

Chilean Alfajores

2/3 cup butter or margarine

1 cup sugar

1 whole egg

2 egg yolks

1 teaspoon vanilla

2 teaspoons grated lemon rind

2-1/2 cups sifted all-purpose flour

1 teaspoon baking powder

1/4 teaspoon salt

1 tablespoon brandy

Preheat oven to 350°F.

1. Cream butter and add sugar gradually beating continually.

2. Add egg and egg yolks and continue beating. Batter should be light and frothy.

3. Mix in vanilla and grated lemon rind.

4. Sift together dry ingredients and add to creamed mixture. Mix well; dough should be smooth.

5. Blend in brandy and chill dough for at least one hour, or longer if necessary. Dough should be firm enough to roll out.

6. On a well floured pastry cloth, roll dough to 1/8-inch thickness and cut into rounds with a 1-1/2-inch cookie cutter.

7. Place on a buttered baking sheet and bake for 15 to 20 minutes or until lightly browned. Remove from oven and allow to cool. Then spread half the cookies with "Dulce de Leche" filling and cover with remaining half, making them into sandwiches.

DULCE DE LECHE

1 can condensed milk

1 cup grated coconut

1. Shake condensed milk well and place opened can in saucepan of water. Boil rapidly for about 1 hour, adding more water as needed.

2. Empty contents into a bowl. Beat with whisk until thickened.

3. Spread the "dulce de leche" or condensed milk on one cookie round and then cover with another round, making a sandwich.

4. Sprinkle coconut on a piece of waxed paper and roll each cookie sandwich on its edge so as to pick up coconut.

Yield: 40 filled cookies

Vanilla Crescents

1 cup butter or
    margarine

1/2 cup
    confectioners' sugar

1 teaspoon vanilla

2-3/4 cups all-purpose
    flour

2/3 cup blanched
    ground almonds

confectioners' sugar

Preheat oven to 350°F.

1. Cream butter and sugar gradually. Stir in vanilla.

2. Sift flour and add along with nuts to butter mixture.

3. Chill dough at least an hour, until it is firm enough to handle.

4. Using one tablespoon of dough for each cookie, roll pieces of dough into 3-inch ropes, then form them into crescents. Place them on an ungreased cookie sheet.

5. Bake for about 20 to 25 minutes.

6. Remove cookies from oven and cool slightly. While still warm, roll them in confectioner's sugar.

Yield: 3-1/2 dozen

Pear Cookies

1/3 cup butter or margarine

1/3 cup sugar

1 teaspoon grated lemon rind

1 egg

1/2 cup ground walnuts

1 cup all-purpose flour

1/4 teaspoon salt

1/2 teaspoon cinnamon

granulated sugar

Preheat oven to 375°F.

1. Cream butter. Add sugar, a small amount at a time, and continue to cream after each addition. Stir in lemon rind.

2. Add egg and ground walnuts and beat well.

3. Sift dry ingredients together and blend gradually into above mixture. When batter is mixed well, chill it for about 1 hour for easy handling.

4. After chilling, shape dough into a long roll about 2 inches thick. Then return it to refrigerator and chill for about 2 hours.

5. Cut cold dough into 1/4-inch-thick slices. Form each slice in a triangular shape of a pear. Taper cookie at end.

6. Place cookies on ungreased baking sheet, flatten a little with hands, and bake for 10 minutes.

7. After baking, sprinkle granulated sugar on each and cool.

Yield: about 5 dozen

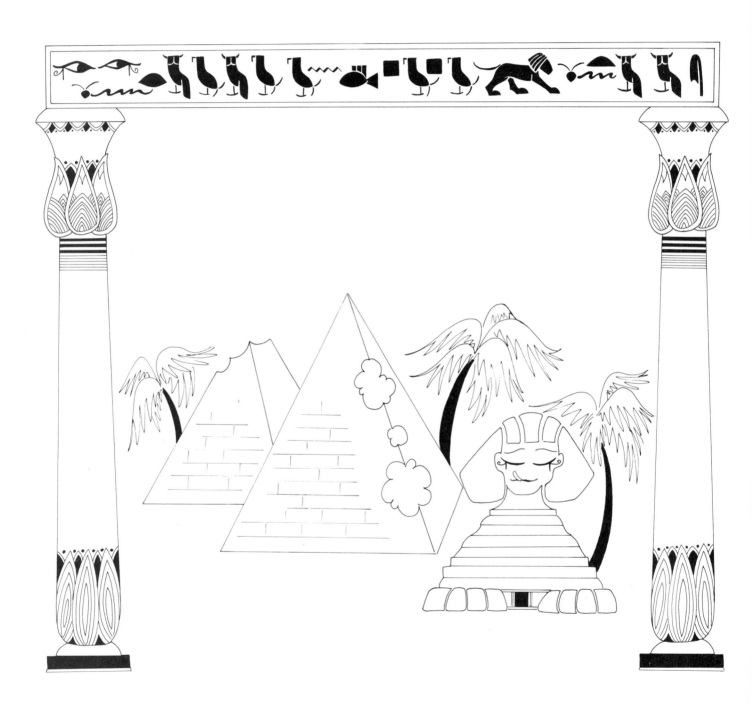

Pyramids

1 cup butter or
margarine

1/2 cup confectioners'
sugar

2 cups flour

1/4 pound almonds,
blanched and slivered

2 teaspoons vanilla

2 tablespoons
confectioners' sugar
sifted

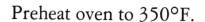

Preheat oven to 350°F.

1. Cream butter and sugar.

2. Add flour and half the almonds. Blend thoroughly. Stir in vanilla. Chill for 15 minutes.

3. Break off pieces of dough about a teaspoonful and place them on ungreased cookie sheet. Press an almond sliver on top of each.

4. Bake for about 20 minutes.

5. Remove cookies from oven and cool. Sprinkle sifted confectioners' sugar over top.

Yield: about 4-1/2 dozen

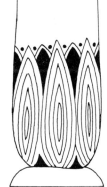
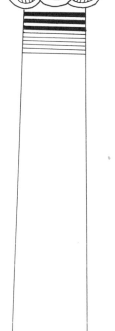
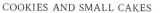

Russian Khvorost

2 eggs

2 tablespoons sugar

2 tablespoons
   salad oil

1 teaspoon vanilla
   extract

2 tablespoons vodka

2 cups all-purpose flour

1/8 teaspoon salt

1/4 teaspoon ground
   cardamom seed

cooking oil

confectioners' sugar

1. Beat eggs; add sugar, oil, and vanilla and mix thoroughly.

2. Add vodka and blend into mixture.

3. Stir in flour, salt and ground cardamom. Then toss dough on lightly floured board and knead well. Add additional small amounts of flour if necessary while kneading until dough no longer sticks to board.

4. Divide dough into four parts and roll each part very thin. Cut with a floured diamond-shaped cooky cutter (3-1/2 inches long). Make a slit about one inch long in the center of each diamond and pull one point through slit like tightening a knot.

5. Heat oil to about 375 degrees and fry until lightly browned (about 2 minutes), turning once.

6. Drain on absorbent paper and sprinkle with confectioners' sugar.

Yield: approximately 5 dozen

Whenever I visited my dear friend Dr. Olga Kissner (who had been, before coming to America, the doctor for the Shah of Iran), I could anticipate being served these delectable morsels. This fine Russian lady taught me to make these one day after we celebrated her eightieth birthday.

Sour Cream Drops

1/4 cup butter or margarine

1/2 teaspoon vanilla

3/4 cup brown sugar

1 egg, beaten

1-1/4 cups all-purpose flour

1/4 teaspoon salt

1/4 teaspoon baking powder

1/2 teaspoon cinnamon

1/2 teaspoon baking soda

1/2 cup sour cream

3/4 cup pitted dates, chopped

1/4 cup chopped walnuts

Preheat oven to 400°F.

1. Cream butter, vanilla, and sugar, until smooth.

2. Add egg and beat well.

3. Measure and mix dry ingredients together. Beginning and ending with dry ingredients, add them to the butter mixture alternately with the sour cream. Stir smooth after each addition.

4. Stir in dates and nuts.

5. Drop teaspoons of batter onto a greased cookie sheet and bake for about 15 minutes.

6. When cookies are cool, frost them.

GOLDEN ICING

1/4 cup butter or margarine

1 cup confectioners' sugar

1/2 teaspoon vanilla

hot water

1. Melt shortening over low heat until golden in color.

2. Stir in sugar and vanilla. Add enough water to make mixture of spreading consistency.

Yield: about 3 dozen

Pretzel Cookies

1/4 pound butter

1/4 cup granulated sugar

1 egg

1 teaspoon vanilla

2 tablespoons
   unsweetened cocoa

3 tablespoons hot water

1-1/2 cups all-purpose
   flour

1/8 teaspoon salt

1. In a large mixing bowl, cream butter and sugar until mixture is light in color.

2. Mix in the egg and vanilla.

3. Dissolve cocoa in hot water and when cool, stir it into the butter mixture.

4. Sift flour and salt and blend into the above mixture a little at a time.

5. Shape dough into a roll about 2 inches wide and 8 inches long. Wrap in waxed paper and refrigerate for at least half an hour, or overnight. Preparations up to this step can be made a day ahead.

Preheat oven to 350°F.

6. Remove dough from refrigerator and slice it crosswise in 1/4-inch slices. Roll each slice in your hand until you have a rope about a foot long. Shape each rope into a pretzel.

7. Arrange the cookies an inch apart on an ungreased cookie sheet and bake them for 10 minutes. Remove cookies from sheet and allow to cool. When they are cool, glaze them.

GLAZE

1/2 cup milk

*1/2 cup semisweet
   chocolate bits*

2/3 cup sugar

1/2 cup light corn syrup

1 teaspoon butter

1. Combine milk, chocolate, sugar, and syrup in top of double boiler and cook over low heat, stirring constantly until sugar is dissolved and chocolate is melted.

2. Stir in butter, remove mixture from heat, and allow it to cool to room temperature.

3. Then, holding the cookies with tongs, dip them into the glaze and allow them to dry on a rack. Be sure to have waxed paper under the rack because the chocolate will drip.

Yield: about 2 dozen pretzels

Swiss Chocolate Squares

DOUGH

1/2 cup butter

1/2 cup sugar

1 egg

2-1/4 cups all-purpose
flour, sifted

1/2 teaspoon baking
powder

1/2 teaspoon salt

1/4 cup milk

1 teaspoon vanilla

1 one-pound can
chocolate syrup

1. Cream butter and sugar thoroughly until mixture is light yellow. Then mix in egg.

2. Sift dry ingredients and add them to the butter mixture, alternating with the milk. Begin and end with dry ingredients.

3. Blend in vanilla and chill dough for about one hour.

Preheat oven to 325 F.

4. When dough is chilled, press into a 9 × 13-inch cookie sheet. Cover entire dough with chocolate syrup and then cover with topping.

TOPPING

3 egg whites

1-1/2 cups confectioners'
　　sugar

1 teaspoon vanilla

1/2 cup finely
　　chopped nuts

1/2 cup grated coconut

4 ounces unsweetened
　　chocolate

1. Place egg whites, sugar and vanilla in top of a double boiler over hot water. Beat egg whites until consistency of marshmallows.

2. Mix in chopped nuts and coconut.

3. Melt chocolate in saucepan and add to beaten egg white mixture.

4. With a spoon, spread topping over syrup until entire cookie sheet is covered.

5. Bake for about 40 minutes.

6. Cool and cut into 1-inch squares.

Yield: about 5 dozen

Leckerle
(A German Christmas Cookie)

3/4 cup honey

2 tablespoons orange juice

3 tablespoons finely diced citron, candied orange and lemon peel

2 teaspoons cinnamon

1 teaspoon crushed cloves

1-1/2 cups confectioners' sugar

1/2 cup chopped walnuts

2 eggs

3 cups all-purpose flour

1/2 teaspoon salt

1 teaspoon baking soda

1. THE DAY BEFORE: in a sauce pan, combine honey and orange juice, bring to a boil, and set aside.

2. In a bowl, combine fruits, spices, sugar, and nuts.

3. Beat eggs and add to fruit mixture in bowl. Stir through. Then add honey mixture and make certain that fruits are well blended with eggs and honey mixture.

4. Sift flour, salt, and baking soda and add to above mixture. Stir thoroughly.

5. Refrigerate mixture overnight in bowl covered with towel or foil.

THE FOLLOWING DAY:

Preheat oven to 350°F.

6. Roll dough out into 1/4-inch thickness and cut with fancy cookie cutters or into 2-inch strips.

7. Bake on an ungreased cookie sheet for 12 minutes.

8. Cookies may be sprinkled with sugar beads for color before baking, or they may be iced with a cream frosting flavored with grated orange and lemon rind or the lemon frosting.

LEMON FROSTING

1 egg white

1/8 teaspoon salt

1-1/4 cup
    confectioners' sugar

2 tablespoons lemon
    juice

1 teaspoon lemon rind

1. Beat egg white and salt.

2. Add sugar alternately with juice.

3. Fold in rind.

Yield: about 5½ dozen

Pies, Puddings, Crêpes and Other Delights

Contents

*B*reathes there a man with soul so dead that he doesn't like pie? Man or woman, pie-haters are few and far between. But there are many who say, "I just can't make pies." I tell you that you can. Practice makes perfect and your money back if it doesn't. Once you relax about the whole thing, you'll roll pies out and together again with ease.

You can even get around pastry shells by using crumb crusts. These can be made from graham crackers, chocolate cookies, ginger snaps or vanilla wafers.

And when it comes to desserts "like mama used to make," there is nothing like the old-fashioned puddings and souffles. Today, people think of a souffle as very-special-occasion, but we used to be able to bet on one whenever my mother had an accumulation of egg whites.

And don't forget

• To prevent fruit pies from becoming soggy, slightly sprinkle crumbs (any kind) on lower crust before adding fruit.
• To seal crusts to keep the juices of fruit pies from escaping, brush the edges of the lower crust with cold water before covering with the top crust. Crimp the edges of the crusts together with the tines of a fork to finish sealing.
• If you cut shortening into flour with your fingers, work quickly so that the warmth of the hands won't melt the shortening. You may also use a pastry blender or food processor. Or take two knives, one in each hand, and cut the fat particles into the flour until they are about the size of a pea.

• Grated cheese sprinkled onto the crust of an apple pie as you're rolling it out gives a new flavor.
• One teaspoon of rum adds a nice flavor to cream pies.
• The volume of beaten egg whites is increased when the eggs are at room temperature.
• The top crust of a fruit pie should be pierced with a fork before baking. The little vents made will allow steam to escape.
• After a double crust fruit pie is assembled, I brush the top with cold milk or cream and then sprinkle on a little brown sugar and a touch of cinnamon.

Never Fail Pie Crust

4 cups all-purpose flour, sifted

2 teaspoons salt

2 tablespoons granulated sugar

1 tablespoon baking powder

1-1/2 cups vegetable shortening

1/2 cup cold water

1 tablespoon vinegar

1 egg, beaten

1. In a bowl place sifted flour, salt, sugar and baking powder.

2. With pastry blender, cut shortening into flour until particles are the size of peas.

3. Mix water, vinegar, and egg in a separate bowl.

4. Add liquid mixture to flour a little at a time, tossing the dough with a fork. Form into a ball and roll in wax paper. refrigerate dough for at least one hour before using. This is enough dough for 4 pie shells or 2 double pies.

5. When ready to use, cut dough into four parts. Take one part, flatten with palm of hand and place between 2 large sheets of wax paper. Then roll out to size of a 9-inch pie.

6. Place rolled dough on pie plate, allowing sides to fall over the rim. Flute edges, cutting away surplus. Prick bottom of shell with fork* and bake in 450 degree oven for about 12 to 15 minutes or until brown.

7. If making a double crust pie, use fresh pieces of wax paper and roll another part for top. Remainder of crust can be saved in refrigerator for another pie as long as a week without spoiling.

* As a reminder—do NOT prick bottom crust when making a fruit or filled pie.

Pie Crust Variations

CHOCOLATE COCONUT CRUST

2 tablespoons butter

2 squares unsweetened
   chocolate

2 tablespoons hot water

2/3 cup sifted
   confectioners' sugar

1-1/3 cups flaked
   coconut

Melt butter and chocolate over low heat until blended. Stir in water and sugar and when smooth, blend in coconut. (Coconut may be toasted for a more interesting flavor.) Press on bottom and sides of a greased 9-inch pie plate and chill until firm.

OATMEAL PIE CRUST

1 cup uncooked
   rolled oats

1/4 cup brown sugar

1/2 cup finely
   chopped nuts

1/3 cup butter or
   margarine, melted

Toast oats in a 350°F. oven for about 10 minutes. Blend with sugar, nuts, and butter. Press on bottom and sides of a 9-inch pie plate. Chill.

CHOCOLATE WAFER PIE CRUST

1-1/4 cups chocolate
wafers, crushed

1 tablespoon
confectioners' sugar

1 teaspoon grated
lemon rind

1/4 cup butter, melted

Combine all ingredients and press on bottom and sides of a 9-inch pie plate.

GRAHAM CRACKER CRUST

1-1/2 cups graham
cracker crumbs

1/3 cup confectioners'
sugar

1/2 cup melted butter

1/2 teaspoon allspice

Blend crumbs, sugar, allspice and melted butter. Pat down on bottom and sides of a 9-inch pie plate to make crust.

Coffee Macaroon Pie

Unbaked 9-inch pie shell
(refer to recipe for
pie crust)

3 eggs, separated

1/4 teaspoon salt

1-1/2 cups sugar

1/4 cup strong cold
coffee

2 tablespoons melted
butter

1 teaspoon lemon juice

1-1/2 cups shredded
coconut

1/2 cup heavy cream,
whipped

Preheat oven to 375°F.

1. Beat egg yolks with salt until thick and lemon colored.

2. Add sugar gradually, beating after each addition.

3. Mix in coffee, butter and lemon juice. Blend thoroughly.

4. Beat egg whites until stiff. Fold in coconut. Then gently fold this mixture into yolk batter.

5. Pour into unbaked pie shell and bake for 50 minutes. Pie is finished when a knife inserted comes out clean. Cool before serving.

6. Garnish with whipped cream.

Blueberry Custard Pie

Baked pie shell (refer to recipe for pie crust on page 106)

1. Line baked pie shell with basic cream filling (recipe below) and cool.

BASIC CREAM FILLING

1/4 cup flour

1/8 teaspoon salt

2 tablespoon cornstarch

1/2 cup sugar

3 eggs, well beaten

2 cups milk, scalded

1 tablespoon butter

1. Mix dry ingredients and add to beaten eggs in the top of a double boiler.

2. Add a very little milk at a time until the mixture is blended. If hot milk is poured into the eggs too quickly they will begin to scramble. Cook in top of double boiler until thick.

3. Mix in the butter and allow mixture to cool before pouring into shell.

BLUEBERRY TOPPING

2 cups fresh blueberries

1/2 cup water

dash of salt

1/2 cup sugar

1/2 teaspoon cinnamon

2-1/2 tablespoons
    cornstarch

2 teaspoons cold water

1 teaspoon lemon juice

1/2 pint heavy cream

2 tablespoons sugar

1 teaspoon vanilla

3/4 cup shredded
    coconut

1. While custard is cooling, wash berries and pick off any small remaining stems. Place in saucepan with water and salt and bring to a boil.

2. Add the sugar and cinnamon and stir through.

3. Make a paste of cornstarch and cold water and add to the berries. Reduce heat to a simmer and continue to cook, stirring constantly, until mixture thickens. Remove from heat.

4. Stir in lemon juice and cool. Then spread over cooled custard filling and refrigerate.

5. Before serving, whip cream and add sugar and vanilla. Then spread over the top of the pie.

6. Sprinkle top with coconut.

Yield: 6 to 8 servings

Chocolate Bar Angel Pie

Preheat oven to 250°F.

3 egg whites

1/4 teaspoon cream of tartar

dash of salt

3/4 cup sugar

1. Have egg whites at room temperature. Add cream of tartar and salt. Beat until frothy. Then gradually add sugar, continuing to beat until whites are shiny and stiff peaks form.

2. On a well buttered 8-inch pie plate, spread meringue on bottom and sides.

3. Bake for about 1 hour. Shell should feel dry to the touch. Remove from oven and cool.

1 six-ounce milk chocolate bar with nuts

2 tablespoons water

3 egg yolks

2 egg whites

1 cup heavy cream

1 teaspoon vanilla

4. In top of double boiler, break candy bar into small pieces. Add water and melt chocolate over hot water. (Do not boil water.) Beat in egg yolks and cool.

5. Beat egg whites stiff and fold into chocolate mixture.

6. Whip cream stiff, add vanilla and fold half into above mixture, reserving the other half for a garnish.

7. Pour filling into cooled shell, spread remaining cream over top and chill overnight. Chopped nuts or chocolate curls may be used for decoration.

Yield: 6 to 8 servings

Fresh Peach Pie

Unbaked pie shell (refer
to recipe for
pie crust)

2 pounds fresh peaches

juice of half lemon

1/2 cup granulated sugar

1/2 cup light brown sugar

3/4 cup water

3 tablespoons cornstarch
mixed with 3 table-
spoons cold water

1/8 teaspoon salt

3 tablespoons bread
crumbs

Preheat oven to 400°F.

1. Place peaches in colander and dip into boiling water for 1 minute.

2. Remove skins and brush peaches with lemon juice. Slice in 1/2-inch pieces.

3. Place sugars and water in a saucepan, add cornstarch and mix well. Cook over medium heat, stirring constantly. When mixture thickens and becomes clear, it is finished.

4. Stir salt into hot mixture and pour over sliced peaches. Mix gently to distribute and allow to cool.

5. Pour peaches into unbaked pie shell that has been sprinkled with bread crumbs.

6. Pie may either be covered with a lattice crust or completely covered with pie dough.

7. Brush upper crust with milk and bake in a 400°F. oven for 40 to 45 minutes.

Fresh Strawberry Pie

Baked pie shell (refer to
recipe for pie crust)

3/4 cup sugar

1/2 cup water

1 quart fresh
strawberries

1/4 teaspoon salt

1-1/2 tablespoons
cornstarch

2 tablespoons cold
water

1 tablespoon lemon juice

1/2 pint heavy cream

2 tablespoons sugar

1 teaspoon vanilla

1. Heat sugar and water in a saucepan until sugar is dissolved.

2. Wash and hull berries. Crush 1 cup of the berries with a fork. Set the remaining berries aside for bottom of pie. Add the crushed berries and salt to the sugar solution. Stir well and bring to a boil. Skim the foam from the top.

3. Make a smooth paste of the cornstarch and water and add to stawberry mixture. Continue cooking until thick. Remove from heat and stir in lemon juice.

4. Place the remaining whole berries on the bottom of baked pie shell and pour the thickened strawberry mixture over the fruit. Refrigerate.

5. Before serving, whip the cream, add the sugar and vanilla, and spread over the top.

Heavenly Cheese Pie

Graham cracker crust
(refer to recipe in
pie crust variations)

1 six-ounce package
semisweet chocolate
bits

1 tablespoon strong
coffee

1 eight-ounce package
cream cheese

1/2 cup light brown
sugar

1/8 teaspoon salt

———

2 eggs, separated

1/4 cup light brown
sugar

1/2 pint heavy cream

1 teaspoon vanilla

1. In top of a double boiler, melt chocolate bits over hot, but NOT BOILING water. Add coffee, stir well and set aside to cool.

2. Allow cheese to stand at room temperature until it softens. Then blend with sugar and salt.

3. Add eggs yolks, one at a time, beating after each addition. Then stir in cooled chocolate.

4. Beat egg whites until stiff but not dry. Slowly add brown sugar and continue to beat until they are stiff and glossy.

5. Whip cream until thick and it holds shape. Fold in vanilla.

6. Fold chocolate mixture into egg white mixture and finally fold in whipped cream.

7. Pour mixture into a graham cracker pie shell and chill in refrigerator.

Yield: 6-8 servings

Raisin Pie

Unbaked 9-inch pie shell
(refer to recipe for
pie crust)

2 eggs

3/4 cup sugar

1 cup sour cream

1 tablespoon flour

dash salt

1/4 teaspoon nutmeg

1/2 teaspoon cinnamon

1 tablespoon grated
lemon rind

1 cup seedless raisins

Preheat oven to 450°F.

1. Beat eggs slightly, stir in sugar and blend in sour cream a small amount at a time.

2. Mix together flour, salt, and seasonings. Stir in raisins, making sure that they are well coated with seasoned flour.

3. Add raisins and seasonings to egg-cream mixture.

4. Pour filling into unbaked pie shell. Bake pie in preheated oven for 10 minutes.

5. Reduce heat to 350° and bake 20 to 30 minutes longer or until a knife inserted in center comes out clean.

Optional: If pie is served cold, it may be garnished with whipped cream.

Yield: 6 servings

Southern Pecan Pie

Unbaked 9-inch pie shell
(refer to recipe for
pie crust)

3 eggs

1 cup dark brown sugar

3/4 cup dark corn syrup

pinch of salt

2 tablespoons dark rum

1/4 cup butter, melted

1 cup pecan halves

1/2 pint heavy cream,
whipped

1 tablespoon rum

Preheat oven to 350°F.

1. Beat eggs until light and fluffy. Stir in sugar, corn syrup and salt.

2. Blend in rum and melted butter. Add pecans.

3. Pour into unbaked pie shell and bake for 40 to 50 minutes or until knife inserted into center comes out clean.

4. Cool pie and serve with rum-flavored whipped cream.

Supreme Marshmallow Pie

Unbaked graham cracker crust (refer to recipe in pie crust variations)

1 pound marshmallows

1 cup milk

1/2 cup crushed pineapple, well drained

3/4 cup chopped walnuts

1 pint heavy cream

2 tablespoons confectioners' sugar

1. Melt marshmallows with milk in top of double boiler. Allow to cool in refrigerator until thick. It takes several hours.

2. Drain pineapple and fold in 1/2 cup of the chopped nuts and distribute evenly. Reserve 1/4 cup for topping. Fold this mixture into cooled marshmallows.

3. Whip cream stiff, add sugar and fold into pineapple-nut mixture.

4. Pour filling into graham cracker crust and top with remaining chopped nuts. Chill before serving.

Yield: 6 servings

English Toffee Cream Pie

CRUMB CRUST

1-1/2 cups vanilla wafer crumbs

2 tablespoons sugar

1/3 cup melted butter

Preheat oven to 350°F.

Make crumbs in a blender or by rolling wafers between sheets of waxed paper with a rolling pin. Blend crumbs, sugar, and melted butter. Press into an even layer against bottom and sides of a 9-inch pie plate. Bake in a preheated oven for 10 minutes. Allow to cool.

FILLING

1/2 pound English toffee or peanut brittle

2 cups heavy cream, whipped

1. Crush toffee or peanut brittle into fine crumbs. Fold crushed brittle into whipped cream.

2. Pour filling into pie shell. Chill thoroughly and serve.

Yield: 6 servings

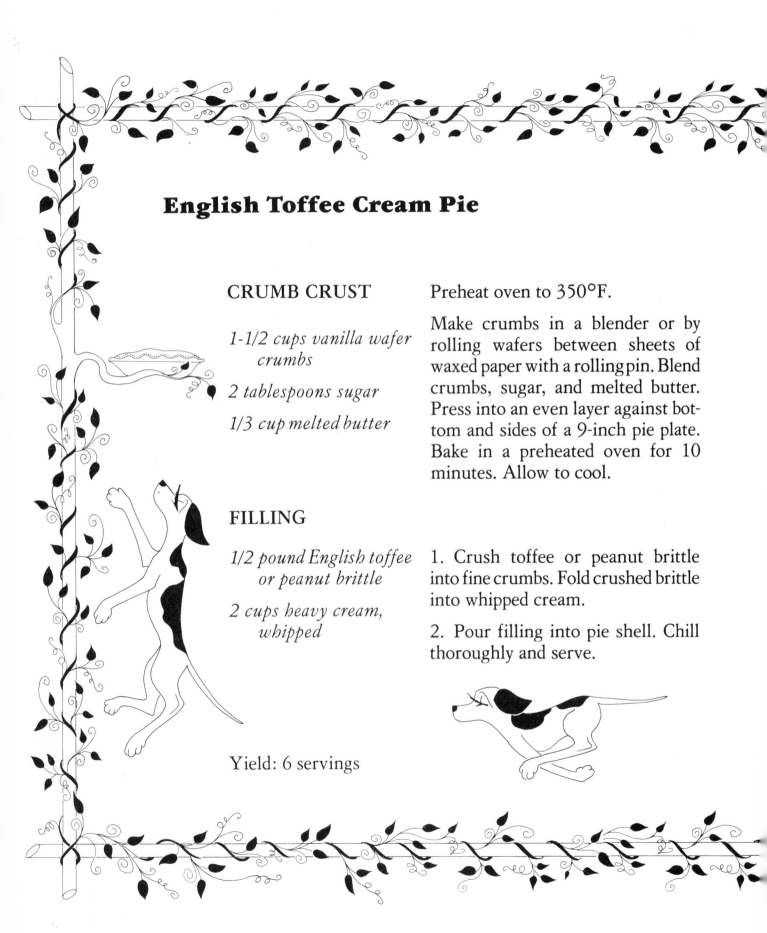

Steamed Chocolate Pudding

2 ounces unsweetened
   chocolate

2 tablespoon butter

2 eggs

1/2 cup sugar

1 teaspoon vanilla

1 cup all-purpose flour

1/8 teaspoon salt

1-1/2 teaspoons baking
   powder

1/2 cup milk

Preheat oven to 350°F.

1. In the top of a double boiler, melt chocolate and butter. Cool.

2. In a bowl mix eggs and sugar until mixture becomes smooth and creamy.

3. Add vanilla and melted chocolate to egg mixture and mix thoroughly.

4. Sift flour, salt, and baking powder together. Then add to above mixture, alternating with milk. Continue to beat until batter is smooth. Then pour into a greased 3-quart pudding mold or ring mold and cover. Place mold on a rack in a kettle. Add boiling water to come halfway up sides of mold and steam in the oven for about 1 hour. If the water evaporates, add more to the bottom of the dish. When pudding is finished, invert mold immediately on hot plate.

5. Serve warm with vanilla sauce from Creole Bread Pudding recipe. (Page 125)

Yield: 6-8 servings

Brazilian Pudim de Coco

1 cup freshly grated
coconut

1/2 cup sugar

6 egg yolks

few whole cloves

Preheat oven to 350°F.

1. Mix grated coconut and sugar. If you are ambitious and coconuts are available, one whole coconut is the correct amount for this recipe. Otherwise, commercial grated coconut will do.

2. To the coconut mixture, add egg yolks one at a time. Stir but do not beat. Then mix in the cloves.

3. Butter a 1-1/2-quart mold, pour in pudding, and place mold in a bain-marie or pan of water.

4. Bake in preheated oven for about 1 hour.

5. When baked, remove from oven and refrigerate until chilled. To serve, slice in portions and accompany with a mild domestic cheese.

Yield: 6 servings

What to do with all of the egg whites? Why, make an angel food cake or meringues. This favorite came from the Brazilian Embassy, where invariably there would be schaum tortes filled with fruit as an alternate dessert. They never wasted the egg whites.

Swiss Rice and Almond Pudding

1 quart milk

3/4 cup long grain rice, washed

1/4 cup sugar

1/4 teaspoon salt

3/4 cup almonds, blanched and chopped

1/4 cup sweet sherry

2 teaspoons vanilla

1/2 pint heavy cream, whipped stiff

1 tablespoon sifted confectioners' sugar

fruit sauce or cherry liqueur

1. In a 2-quart saucepan, bring milk to a boil and add rice, sugar, and salt.

2. Cook rice over low heat for about 25 minutes or until the rice is soft. To test for softness, take some rice between thumb and forefinger. If there is no hard kernel in the center, the rice is done. Be cautious not to allow rice to become mushy.

3. Pour finished rice into a shallow bowl so that it will cool quickly.

4. After rice is cool, add chopped nuts, sherry, and vanilla.

5. Whip cream with confectioners' sugar. When above mixture is sufficiently cool, fold in whipped cream.

6. Put pudding into your serving dish and chill before serving.

7. A cold raspberry or cherry sauce served on top of the rice dessert adds an interesting flavor.

Yield: about 4 servings

FRUIT SAUCE

To make a fruit sauce, use any flavorful fruit juice, add a squeeze of lemon and bring to a boil. To thicken: for every cup of juice add 1 teaspoon cornstarch dissolved in cold water. Continue to boil, stirring constantly until sauce is slightly thickened. Add a little sugar if not sweet enough.

Creole Bread Pudding

1/4 loaf French bread

1/2 teaspoon baking
powder

1/4 teaspoon salt

1/2 cup raisins

1 tablespoon butter

2 cups milk, scalded

2 eggs, separated

1/2 cup sugar

2 tablespoons sugar

Preheat oven to 350°F.

1. Cut or break bread into bite size squares and spread over buttered pan or casserole.

2. Combine baking powder and salt and sprinkle over raisins. Then distribute raisins over bread cubes. Dot top with butter.

3. Pour scalded milk over bread.

4. Beat egg yolks and sugar and pour over milk-soaked bread.

5. Beat egg whites until frothy. Add sugar and continue beating until stiff. Spread over top of bread mixture and bake in 350°F. oven for 40 minutes.

6. Serve hot with vanilla sauce.

VANILLA SAUCE

1 tablespoon butter

2 tablespoons flour

2 cups boiling water

1/4 cup sugar

1 teaspoon vanilla

1. Melt butter in saucepan and stir in flour until it bubbles.

2. Add boiling water and sugar. Boil until smooth and slightly thickened.

3. Blend in vanilla and strain sauce. Serve hot.

Yield: 4-6 servings

Persimmon Pudding

1 cup sugar

1 cup all-purpose flour

2 teaspoons soda

1 teaspoon cinnamon

1/2 teaspoon salt

1 egg, beaten

1/4 cup melted butter

1/3 cup milk

scant cup persimmon pulp (strained and very ripe)

1/2 cup chopped nuts (optional)

Preheat oven to 375°F.

1. Sift dry ingredients.

2. Combine beaten egg, melted butter, milk and pulp. (It takes about 2 large or 3 medium persimmons.) Pulp may be scooped out of shell and pureed in blender.

3. Stir dry ingredients into persimmon mixture. Add nuts.

4. Generously grease and flour a 4-cup pudding mold or casserole. Pour mixture into mold, cover, and put on rack in kettle. Add boiling water to come half-way up sides of mold.

5. Steam in preheated oven for about 75 to 90 minutes, until tested done (like a cake—should be dry).

6. Remove from oven, uncover, and knock out on a rack. This may be served warm with hard sauce (below).

Yield: 8 servings

HARD SAUCE

1/2 cup butter

2 cups sifted
   confectioners' sugar

2 teaspoons boiling
   water

1 teaspoon vanilla

1 tablespoon brandy

Cream butter and add sugar gradually. Add water and beat until creamy. Add flavors. May chill until ready to use, but serve at room temperature.

Yield: about 2-1/2 cups.

Orange Custard Pudding

2 medium eating oranges

2 tablespoons sugar

_____

1 cup sugar

4 eggs, separated

1/4 cup sifted all-
purpose flour

2 cups scalded milk

1 teaspoon vanilla

1 tablespoon grated
orange rind

pinch of salt

1 tablespoon sugar

Preheat oven to 400°F.

1. Peel and section oranges. Remove membrane and add sugar.

2. Beat sugar into egg yolks slowly and continue to beat until color is light. Then beat in flour.

3. Very gradually pour scalded milk into yolk mixture, stirring constantly. Pour into saucepan and heat over low flame until sauce thickens. Stir with wire whisk to prevent scorching.

4. Stir in vanilla and grated rind; turn into a 2-quart casserole.

5. Drain off juice from orange sections and place them into custard.

6. Beat egg whites and salt until soft peaks form. Then sprinkle in sugar and beat until stiff. Spread over custard and bake in 400°F. oven until peaks are delicately brown, about 8 minutes. Chill and serve cold.

Yield: 4-6 servings

This may be served as a plain custard, leaving out the orange sections, or flavored with bananas and/or coconut.

Basic Crêpe Recipe

1 scant cup flour

3 eggs

dash salt

1 cup milk

2 tablespoons melted
  butter

———

Optional:

2 teaspoons sugar

1 tablespoon cognac

1 teaspoon vanilla

1. Blend all the ingredients in blender. Consistency should be like light cream. If you do not have a blender, beat with a wire whisk.

2. For a dessert crêpe, add the sugar, cognac and vanilla.

3. Allow batter to stand covered for 1 to 2 hours in refrigerator before using. If the mixture has become thick, stir in a few tablespoons of milk to get the right consistency.

4. Heat a 6-inch skillet and brush with a vegetable fat or clarified butter.

5. Pour in about 3 tablespoons of the batter and tilt the pan so that the entire bottom is covered. When the sides pull away from the pan, turn it over and cook for another minute. This must be done quickly and caution must be taken not to overcook, otherwise the crêpes will be too dry.

6. Turn the crêpe out on a towel. Continue same way, greasing skillet each time, until all of the batter is used.

Yield: about 10 crêpes

Crêpes with Poached Apricots

6 crêpes at room
   temperature

6 canned apricot halves

juice of apricots

1/4 cup ground nuts

2 tablespoons
   confectioners' sugar

2 tablespoons melted
   butter

1/3 cup brandy, warmed

Preheat oven to 350°F.

1. Make crêpes from basic crêpe recipe.

2. Peel apricots and warm through with some of the juice.

3. Fill crêpes with drained, warm apricots, placing fruit in center of crêpe. Then fold sides to center and top and bottom to meet, like an envelope.

4. Mix ground nuts and sugar and sprinkle tops of crêpes generously with nut-sugar mixture.

5. Arrange crêpes in a baking dish and drizzle melted butter over tops.

6. Place in a preheated 350°F. oven for about 30 minutes before serving.

7. When ready to serve, pour warmed brandy over hot crêpes and light with match. Bring to table aflame.

Yield: 6 servings

Crêpes with Strawberries

1 quart fresh
   strawberries

1/4 cup kirsch

1/4 cup orange flavored
   liqueur

4 teaspoons granulated
   sugar

1 quart French vanilla
   ice cream

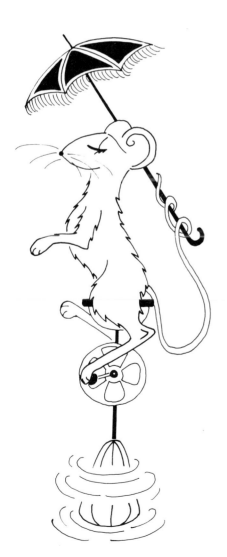

1. Wash and hull strawberries. Measure one cup of the berries and set aside for a garnish.

2. Mash the remaining berries and heat through in a chafing dish or a skillet. Then mix in the kirsch, orange liqueur, and sugar. Warm through and light with a match. While the puree is flaming, stir several times until flame dies down.

3. Place 6 dessert crêpes (see basic crêpe recipe) folded into quarters, into the sauce and simmer for a few minutes, basting with the sauce.

4. Put one scoop of ice cream in each dessert dish. Place a few of the reserved berries around the ice cream and cover the ice cream with a crêpe. Then spoon some of the warm sauce over each crêpe.

Yield: about 10 servings

GREEK BAKLAVA

22 sheets commercial filo dough

1-1/2 cups clarified butter

1 cup ground almonds

1 cup ground walnuts

1/2 cup sugar

1 teaspoon cinnamon

Preheat oven to 300°F.

1. Melt butter.

2. Mix nuts, sugar, and cinnamon together.

3. With a pastry brush, coat bottom of a 10 × 15-inch pastry sheet with melted butter. Line with filo sheet, brush with melted butter, and continue until you have layered 6 sheets.

4. Distribute one fourth of nut mixture over top and then continue with four sheets, drizzling butter over each sheet. Repeat with one-fourth of nut mixture, topping with sheets drizzled with butter. Continue in this manner.

5. Finish with 4 sheets of filo as top crust.

6. Cut into 2-inch diamond shapes.

7. Drip remaining butter on top and bake in preheated oven for about 1-1/2 hours or until golden brown.

8. Cover with syrup. (See next page)

SYRUP

1 cup honey

2 cups sugar

2-1/4 cups water

1 teaspoon lemon juice

1 teaspoon grated
   lemon rind

1. Boil all ingredients in a saucepan for about 5 minutes until mixture becomes syrupy.

2. Allow to stand until cool. Then pour over entire baklava. Allow baklava to stand for 2 hours before serving.

Baklava is a celebrated Greek pastry and baked, in true Greek tradition, for happy events such as weddings, engagements, and christenings.

A word to the wise: filo leaves should be kept in the refrigerator until ready to be used. Do not open package until fillings are ready. As you work with them, keep them covered with waxed paper and a damp cloth because the minute the leaves hit the air they turn brittle and break into flakes.

Armenian Lokma

4 eggs

1/4 teaspoon salt

1 cup yogurt or
  sour cream

2 cups all-purpose
  flour

1 tablespoon sugar

3 teaspoons baking
  powder

3 teaspoons baking soda

1 pint cooking oil

syrup or sifted
  confectioners' sugar

1. Beat eggs, salt, and yogurt together.

2. Measure and sift dry ingredients together. Add to egg mixture and mix well.

3. Heat oil in a deep pan until it is hot enough to sizzle when a drop of water is sprinkled on it. Gently drop one tablespoonful of dough mixture at a time into hot oil. Turn so that both sides are browned.

4. Serve warm with syrup or sprinkle with confectioners' sugar.

Yield: about 2 dozen

Mama's Apple Kugel

PIE CRUST

Pastry for two-crust pie (refer to recipe for pie crust)

Preheat oven to 450°F.

Roll half of the pie pastry very thin. Slightly butter an 8-inch oblong pyrex dish or cake tin. Lay the rolled crust into the baking dish so that some of the crust overlaps the sides.

FILLING

3 pounds baking apples

3/4 cup granulated sugar

1/4 cup brown sugar

1 teaspoon cinnamon

1/4 teaspoon nutmeg

1 tablespoon flour

*1 ten-ounce jar of
    strawberry or
    raspberry jelly*

3 tablespoons butter

*2 tablespoons milk or
    cream*

*1 tablespoon brown
    sugar*

Preheat oven to 450°F.

1. Peel, core, and thinly slice apples. Arrange half of the sliced apples over the bottom crust.

2. Mix sugars with other dry ingredients and sprinkle half this mixture over the apples.

3. Make another layer of apples and sprinkle the other half of the sugar mixture over it.

4. Dab teaspoons of jam over the top of the apples.

5. Dot the entire top with butter.

6. Roll out the other half of the pastry and cover the pie. Pinch the edges and prick the top in 4 or 5 places with a fork to allow the steam to escape.

7. Brush upper crust with milk or cream and then sprinkle a small amount of brown sugar over it.

8. Bake in preheated oven for 15 minutes. Then reduce heat to 350° and bake for 35 minutes more. Apples should be juicy and crust brown.

9. Remove from oven and cut in squares. Serve hot or cool.

Yield: 10 servings

Lemon Soufflé

3 tablespoons flour

3/4 cup milk

1/2 cup sugar

4 egg yolks, beaten

juice and grated rind
of 1 lemon

2 tablespoons butter

5 egg whites

dash of salt

1/4 teaspoon cream of
tartar

2 teaspoons granulated
sugar

whipped cream, optional

Preheat oven to 375°F.

1. In a saucepan, beat 1/4 cup milk with flour until well blended. Add remaining milk and sugar. Stir over medium heat until mixture thickens.

2. Stir a little hot mixture into beaten egg yolks. Add juice, rind of lemon, and butter. Return yolk mixture to pan and blend.

3. Beat egg whites until slightly frothy. Add salt, cream of tartar and continue to beat. Add sugar and beat until stiff peaks are formed.

4. STIR about 3 tablespoons of beaten egg white into lemon mixture. Then carefully fold in remainder of beaten egg whites.

5. Butter and sprinkle sugar on bottom and sides of an 8-quart soufflé dish. Pour in soufflé, allowing about 1-1/2-inch space from top.

6. Bake in preheated oven for about 30 to 35 minutes. Top of soufflé should be brown and a testing needle should come out clean when inserted in center.

7. Serve immediately. Thickly whipped and sweetened cream may be served from a separate bowl.

Yield: makes 6 servings

Cheese Blintzes

FILLING

8 ounces dry cottage
cheese

8 ounces cream cheese

1 egg, beaten

dash of salt

2 tablespoons sugar

1/4 teaspoon cinnamon

BATTER

4 eggs

1/4 teaspoon salt

1-1/2 cups milk

2 tablespoons melted
butter

1-1/4 cups all-purpose
flour

melted butter

1. Mix filling ingredients and set aside.

2. Pour batter ingredients into a blender and blend until smooth. If electric mixer is used, add flour to other ingredients. Consistency should be like cream.

3. Grease 7-inch skillet on bottom and sides. When skillet sizzles to drop of water, pour in about 3 tablespoons batter, tilting pan from side to side so that batter covers bottom. Cook lightly until pancake begins to pull away from sides of skillet. If batter thickens, a small amount of milk may be added to adjust consistency.

4. Spread clean towel on counter and knock out pancake to cool.

5. As each pancake cools, place a generous tablespoon filling in center. Fold sides to center and roll like jelly roll. Put aside to make room for other pancakes as they are being made. Grease skillet slightly after each time. When ready to serve brown in butter in a skillet or they may be baked in a buttered dish in a low oven until light brown.

Yield: about 24 blintzes

The wrappers or pancakes may be made in advance and refrigerated for no more than two days. They should be completely cool and separated by sheets of waxed paper, stacked and carefully covered with waxed paper and then wrapped in towel.

They may also be frozen, with or without filling, but packaged flat and airtight.

Fruit Desserts

Contents

*F*ruits offer a great variety of desserts and flavors. They need to be treated, however, with the same care and understanding one takes in the preparation of delicate pastries or yeast doughs.

And don't forget

• Peeled fresh apples, peaches, pears or bananas can be prevented from darkening by dipping them in orange, lemon or grapefruit juice. The leftover juice can be saved for a simple salad dressing.

• Three to four medium-sized apples will make one and a half cups of applesauce.

• Prick the skin of a raw apple before baking to prevent splitting.

• Apricots should be sweetened during the last five minutes of cooking. If the sugar is added sooner, they will toughen.

• Peel citrus fruits or pineapple over a bowl to catch the juices.

• Fruit preserves or jams to be rubbed through a sieve should be heated first.

• The kiwi, a cute, furry brown oval about the size of a lemon, is delicate but firm inside. Its green meat is sprinkled with tiny, edible black seeds.

• Early peaches are the most luscious. To ripen them, store in a paper bag in a dark place for a day or two.

• Wintertime pears:

Anjou (pronounced "onjoo") has a green-yellow skin when ripe and is sweet, juicy and creamy white.

Bosc has a russet brown skin and is sweet. It is excellent for baking.

Comice (pronounced "cum ees") is plump in shape and is yellow-green with a red blush. It is often called the Christmas pear.

• Pears will ripen rapidly in a paper bag at room temperature.

• Three to four persimmons will ripen in a plastic bag along with an apple. Persimmons are not ripe until they are mushy.

• Plums, grown in more than 100 varieties, can be divided into two main types. The European type is blue or purple, medium-sized and mild in flavor. The Japanese type is generally medium to large and very juicy with a red or yellow skin.

• Plums will turn from ripe to overripe faster than almost any other fruit.

• Strawberries should be used as soon as possible after buying. Hull them *after* washing and serve at room temperature.

Apples Flambé

6 large baking apples

1/4 cup raisins

1/4 chopped nuts

1/2 cup brown sugar

1-1/4 cups white wine —
3/4 cup to be used
in baking

1 tablespoon sugar

1 tablespoon brandy

1 cube sugar

2 tablespoons heated
brandy

Preheat oven to 350°F.

1. Peel and core 6 large baking apples. Combine raisins and nuts and fill each center with a heaping teaspoonful of mixture, saving the remainder to be used later.

2. Arrange apples in a large baking pan and sprinkle each with brown sugar. Pour 3/4 cup wine into the pan and bake for about 50 minutes or until tender and almost mushy. Add more wine or water if needed.

3. When apples are finished, remove them to a warm platter. Add remainder of raisin-nut mixture plus other half-cup wine to syrup in the pan. Return pan to oven and cook for 10 minutes so that sauce is warmed through. Pour over apples on platter.

4. Sprinkle a little sugar and brandy over each apple.

5. Place lump of sugar in a large spoon, pour heated brandy over and ignite with a match. Pour over apples while spoon is in flame.

Yield: 6 servings

Apricot Cream with Brandied Grapes

8 ounces dried
   apricots

1 teaspoon lemon juice

1 teaspoon grated
   lemon rind

2 egg yolks

1 cup confectioners'
   sugar, sifted

dash of salt

1/4 teaspoon vanilla

1/2 pint heavy cream

1. Wash and cook apricots in small amount of water until tender, about 35-40 minutes.

2. Puree apricots in blender. Stir in lemon juice and rind and cool.

3. Beat egg yolks and sifted sugar together. Add salt and vanilla and blend until smooth.

4. Fold apricot puree into egg yolk mixture.

5. Whip cream stiff and gently fold into apricot mixture. Cover and chill for at least three hours.

6. When ready to serve, mound strained brandied grapes over top.

BRANDIED GRAPES

1/2 pound dark grapes

1/4 cup brandy

1. Seed grapes and cut in half.

2. Sprinkle brandy over grapes and toss lightly. Chill for about 2 hours. Turn occasionally so brandy flavor is absorbed.

Yield: 8 servings

Blushed Poached Peaches

6 firm ripe peaches

1/2 cup sugar

1 tablespoon butter

1 package frozen
raspberries, thawed

juice and grated rind of
one orange

1/3 cup brandy or cognac

1. Plunge peaches into boiling water. Slide off skins and cut in halves.

2. In a chafing dish or large skillet, heat sugar and butter over low heat until mixture caramelizes.

3. Puree raspberries in blender and add to caramelized sauce.

4. Add orange juice and grated rind to above mixture and blend through. Allow sauce to bubble.

5. Roll each peach half around in sauce until completely coated.

6. Heat brandy in a small saucepan and ignite with a match. Pour flaming liqueur over peaches.

7. Baste peaches with sauce until flame dies down. Serve in individual dishes with hot sauce poured over peach.

Yield: 6 servings

Baked Pears with Apricot Sauce Topping

1/2 cup macaroon
    crumbs

6 medium Bartlett pears

1/2 cup apricot preserves

1/2 cup sherry

1/4 cup chopped walnuts

1/4 cup butter

1. SOME TIME BEFORE: Dry macaroons in a 200°F. oven. Pulverize in blender.

Preheat oven to 350°F.

2. Wash, core, and cut pears into lengthwise slices about 1/4 inch thick.

3. Arrange slices in a buttered baking dish to make overlapping layers.

4. Stir sherry into preserves and warm through. Pour over pears.

5. Sprinkle crumbs and nuts over pears and dot with butter.

6. Bake for about half an hour until tops are brown. Serve immediately.

Yield: 6 servings

148

Strawberries Romanoff

1 quart strawberries

1/2 cup orange liqueur

juice of 1/2 medium
orange

1 cup heavy cream

1 pint French vanilla
ice cream

1. Wash and hull strawberries. Sprinkle with sugar if berries are not sweet. Pour liqueur and juice over and allow to marinate for about one hour.

2. Whip cream until stiff. Let ice cream become slightly soft. Then fold whipped cream into ice cream.

3. Carefully fold marinated strawberries into the cream mixture, reserving 6 berries for decoration.

4. Fill parfait glasses or large bowl with the dessert and arrange remaining strawberries on top. Serve at once.

Yield: 6 servings

During strawberry season, don't miss the opportunity to make this. A hint: take the dessert out of the freezer and place it in the lower part of the refrigerator about the time you begin to eat or it will be too frozen to eat at serving time.

Compote de Cerise

2 quarts fresh
   strawberries

2 boxes frozen
   raspberries. thawed

3 tablespoons grated
   orange rind

1. Wash and hull berries. Drain off all water.

2. Puree raspberries in blender. Strain to remove seeds.

3. Sprinkle orange rind over strawberries and then top with pureed raspberries.

4. Chill.

Yield: 8 servings

A variation is to use several tablespoons Cointreau or any orange flavored liqueur in place of the grated orange rind. It adds an interesting flavor.

Coconut-Pineapple Chunks in Apricot Nectar

2 sixteen-ounce cans
　apricot juice

juice of 2 lemons,
　strained

2 cups heavy cream

1 medium size fresh
　pineapple,
　　　　or
1 twenty-ounce can
　pineapple chunks,
　drained

2 four-ounce cans
　grated coconut

1. Combine apricot juice and strained lemon juice. Whip cream stiff and blend in juice.

2. If using fresh pineapple, peel, core and cut into one-inch squares. Sprinkle generously with sugar and allow to stand for one or two hours. Then drain off juice.

3. Roll pineapple chunks in the grated coconut. Place pieces in a large crystal bowl to be passed separately from the flavored whipped cream which is used as a sauce for the pineapple.

Yield: 6 servings

Carmelized Applesauce Mold

12 to 14 medium
    cooking apples

———

1/2 cup sugar

2 tablespoons water

———

1/2 teaspoon cinnamon

5 tablespoons sugar

1 tablespoon grated
    lemon peel

1/4 cup rum

1/4 cup butter

4 eggs, separated

whipped cream,
    sweetened

Preheat oven to 400°F.

1. Peel, core and slice apples. There should be about 10 cups. Cover and cook in a large saucepan over very low heat for about 20 minutes, until tender, stirring occasionally.

2. To caramelize mold, boil sugar with water in a saucepan over moderate heat until syrup is caramelized. Shake pan in a circular motion while boiling. When syrup is ready, pour into 6 × 3-inch mold, tilt in all directions so bottom and sides are coated with caramel. Dip mold in cold water for 2 to 3 seconds. After caramel has stopped running, turn mold upside down over a plate.

3. Stir cinnamon, sugar, and grated lemon peel into applesauce. Then increase heat and boil for a few minutes, stirring, until apples become a thick puree. This should make about 4 cups applesauce.

4. Remove from heat, stir in rum, add butter and mix through. One by one, beat in egg yolks and finally fold in beaten egg whites.

5. Pour apple mixture into caramelized mold.

6. Cover filled caramelized mold with a lid, set into a pan of boiling water that comes up to level of apple mixture, and bake in oven for 1 to 1-1/2 hours. The water should simmer slightly. When filling begins to shrink from sides of mold, it is finished.

7. Remove from oven and water, cool, reverse onto a serving dish. This may be served as a cold dessert as well. Refrigerate overnight and serve with flavored whipped cream.

Yield: 6 servings

Glazed Bananas Flambé

6 bananas

juice of 1/2 lemon, strained

1/2 teaspoon salt

3 tablespoons butter

1 cup plum wine (NOT port)

1 cup brown sugar

1/4 teaspoon ground cloves

1/2 tablespoon grated orange rind

1/2 teaspoon cinnamon

1/2 teaspoon nutmeg

3/4 cup grated coconut

1/4 cup finely chopped almonds

6 tablespoons heavy dark rum, heated

Preheat oven to 375°F.

1. Peel and cut bananas in half; cut each half lengthwise. Sprinkle each piece with juice to prevent darkening.

2. Season bananas with a sprinkle of salt and sauté lightly in butter.

3. In a separate saucepan, make a syrup of the wine, brown sugar, and seasonings and cook for several minutes over low heat.

4. Place bananas in a buttered casserole and cover with the spiced syrup.

5. Then sprinkle grated coconut and chopped almonds over the bananas.

6. Bake about 10 minutes, or until topping is browned.

7. Just before serving, pour the heated rum over the bananas. Ignite with a match and serve.

Yield: 6 servings

The first 5 steps of preparation may be made before dinner. Then while you are eating, preheat oven and bake the bananas so they will be ready for a flaming finish!

Hawaiian Papaya Frost

3 papayas

3 oranges

1-1/2 cups sugar

1-1/2 pints yogurt or
commercial sour
cream

1/4 teaspoon salt

juice of 1 medium lemon

1/2 pint heavy cream,
whipped

1/2 cup flaked coconut

1. Peel, seed, and slice papayas. Peel and cut oranges in pieces. Combine with sugar and whirl in blender until smooth.

2. Combine yogurt, salt, and lemon juice. Add fruit mixture. Freeze in a freezer container.

3. One hour before serving, transfer from freezer to refrigerator. Portion about 1/2 to 3/4 cup into each dessert dish. Top with whipped cream and coconut. Garnish with papaya slices if desired.

Yield: makes 12 servings

The refreshing taste and texture suggests a sherbet.

Hot Fruit Compote

12 macaroons, crumbled

4 cups assorted canned fruits, like peaches, pears, apricots, or pineapple, drained

1/4 cup brown sugar

1/2 cup almonds, slivered and toasted

1/2 cup sweet sherry

1/4 cup melted butter

1. SOME TIME BEFORE: Dry 12 macaroons in a 200°F. oven. Pulverize in blender.

Preheat oven to 350°F.

2. Butter a 2-1/2-quart casserole. Cover the bottom with a portion of the macaroon crumbs.

3. Spread assorted fruits on top of crumb layer. Then continue, alternating layers of macaroon crumbs with fruit and finish with crumbs.

4. Sprinkle brown sugar and toasted almonds over the top of your last layer of crumbs. Then drizzle with sherry.

5. Bake uncovered for 30 minutes. When compote is removed from oven, pour melted butter over it and serve hot.

Yield: 8 servings

Any assortment of canned fruits can be used. A variety, however, lends interest in taste, texture, and color. If you do not have sherry, brandy will serve as a good substitute. A bowl of sweetened whipped cream at the table adds a nice touch if you are not a calorie watcher.

Limed Rainbow Fruit

1 small cantaloupe

1/2 honeydew melon

1/8 small watermelon

1 cup fresh blueberries, washed

2/3 cup sugar

1/3 cup water

1 teaspoon grated lime rind

6 tablespoons lime juice

1/2 cup light rum

1. Cut melons in half, remove seeds, and with melon scoop, form fruit into small balls.

2. Place melon balls and blueberries into a serving bowl and chill in refrigerator for at least 1 hour.

3. Mix sugar and water in a small saucepan, bring to boil, and simmer for about 5 minutes.

4. Then add grated lime rind to sugar solution and let cool to room temperature.

5. Stir lime juice and rum into the syrup mixture and pour over the melon balls and berries. Then cover and refrigerate for several hours. More rum can be added, depending on your taste.

Yield: 6 servings

Grapes Jill

1 pound seedless
   green grapes

1/2 cup sour cream

1 tablespoon crème
   de cacao

1 pint fresh raspberries

1. Wash, stem and pat dry all the grapes.

2. Mix sour cream and crème de cacao and pour over the grapes.

3. Wash and dry raspberries.

4. Chill the fruit in separate bowls and when ready to serve, place creamed grapes in a shallow dish and surround them with raspberries.

Yield: 6 servings

Mished Fruits

1 medium-sized ripe
  pineapple

1 medium eating apple

1 large navel orange

2 bananas, sliced

1/4 pound Bing
  cherries, pitted

1 pint fresh strawberries

3/4 cup orange liqueur

1/2 cup grated coconut

1 pint sour cream

1. Pare the pineapple and apple and cut them bite size.

2. Peel orange and cut in half crosswise. Section the halves, loosening and removing each segment into bowl with pineapple and apple pieces. Add remaining juice to bowl.

3. Add bananas and cherries to fruit, carefully stirring through so that the banana slices are covered with the juice to prevent darkening.

4. Wash and hull strawberries and add to other fruit.

5. Mix orange liqueur through and chill for several hours.

6. When ready to serve, stir fruit through once again and sprinkle with the coconut.

7. A side dish of sour cream may be served for those who like that combination.

Yield: 6 servings

Delights of Paris

16 *paper cupcake cups*

12 *ounces semisweet chocolate chips or chocolate bars*

12 *champagne biscuits or finger-shaped butter cookies*

3 *tablespoons kirsch*

1 *pint fresh strawberries, cut up and sugared to taste*

1 *pint fresh raspberries, sugared*

1 *cup heavy cream*

2 *tablespoons sugar*

1 *teaspoon vanilla*

1. Set double thickness cupcake paper cups into a muffin tin (to make 8 cups).

2. Melt chocolate in a double boiler over hot water, cool slightly, and spoon 2 tablespoons into each paper cup. With the back of the spoon, spread the chocolate evenly over the bottom and sides of the cup. Do not allow it to run over the edge.

3. Chill until firm. Carefully remove the paper cups and chill again.

4. While the remaining chocolate is still soft in the saucepan and after the cups have been made, take 4 biscuits, break them in half, and dip one end of each into the chocolate. Let them harden while the cups are still in the refrigerator.

5. When you are ready to serve dessert, crumble one biscuit into each chocolate

(next page)

cup. Sprinkle with kirsch and top with a layer of strawberries.

6. Over each layer of strawberries, place sugared raspberries.

7. Whip cream until it gets thick. Add sugar and vanilla; continue to beat until stiff. Spoon some of the whipped cream over each cup and garnish with a slice of strawberry or a raspberry, whichever you prefer.

8. Immediately before serving, garnish with the half biscuit that has had one end dipped into the chocolate.

Yield: 8 servings

The cups may be made ahead and kept in the freezer until ready to be used. They are fragile and must be packed carefully. Believe me, this is a delight. When we were in Paris, I was lucky to get this recipe in a tiny restaurant on the Left Bank.

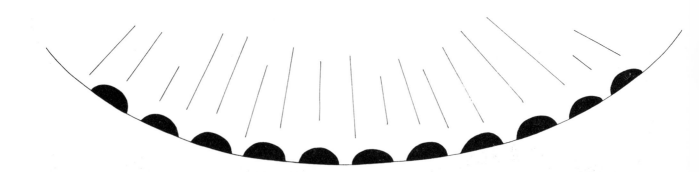

Sherried Apricot Whip

8 ounces dried apricots

1/2 cup sugar

1/2 cup sweet sherry

2 egg whites

1/4 cup sugar

1/2 cup heavy cream, whipped

1 tablespoon grated orange rind

1. In a saucepan, soak the apricots in water for several hours.

2. Stir in sugar and cook apricots over low heat until tender, about 20 minutes.

3. Drain the apricots and cook remaining syrup until it forms a thick glaze. Stir the glaze into the apricots and cool.

4. Add sherry and rub mixture through sieve or puree in blender.

5. Beat egg whites slightly and gradually add sugar until the whites hold their shape. Fold into the apricot puree. Add orange rind.

Yield: 6 servings

Orange Whip in Orange Shells

8 orange halves

1-3/4 cups fresh or
frozen orange juice
strained

1/4 cup orange liqueur

grated rinds of half a
lemon and 3 oranges

6 eggs, separated

1/2 cup sugar

1/2 tablespoon
cornstarch

1/8 teaspoon salt

2 tablespoons sugar

1/2 cup heavy cream

1 ounce semisweet
chocolate

1. Scoop out orange shells, scraping out the tough fibers. The edges can be cut in scallops for a more attractive appearance. Keep wrapped in a moist towel in refrigerator until ready to be filled.

2. Measure and strain orange juice and liqueur into a container and add rind.

3. In a mixing bowl beat egg yolks, gradually adding sugar. Continue to beat until color is a pale yellow.

4. Dissolve cornstarch in the orange juice mixture and beat it into the yolks.

5. Pour into a saucepan over a low flame and heat slowly, stirring constantly until the mixture thickens slightly. Care should be taken not to permit sauce to come to a simmer. Then remove from heat and give it several vigorous stirrings.

6. In a separate bowl, beat the egg whites and salt until soft peaks form. Gradually sprinkle in the sugar and beat until stiff peaks are formed.

7. Fold egg whites into the hot mixture and chill. While the custard is chilling, fold the mixture once or twice to maintain the custardy texture.

8. Whip the cream stiff and fold into the custard. Fill orange shells and chill overnight.

9. Grate chocolate over each shell before serving.

Yield: 8 servings

Prune Fluff

1/2 cup macaroon
    crumbs

1 eight-ounce package
    dried prunes

3 tablespoons sweet
    sherry

4 egg whites

1/4 teaspoon salt

1/2 cup ground walnuts

2 teaspoon lemon juice

1 teaspoon grated
    lemon rind

1. SOMETIME AHEAD: Dry 12 macaroons in a 200°F. oven. Pulverize in blender.

Preheat oven to 350°F.

2. Cover prunes with water and cook until tender. Remove prunes from juice, pit, and puree in blender.

2. Mix in sherry and crumbs.

3. Beat egg whites with salt until stiff. Then carefully fold in ground nuts, lemon juice, and grated rind.

4. Fold whites into prune puree.

5. Butter a 4-cup casserole and carefully spoon in the prune mixture.

6. Place in a shallow pan of water and bake for about 25 minutes. Cool and chill.

Yield: 6 servings

Poached Pears with Crème Anglaise

6 pears, slightly
   underripe

juice of 1/2 lemon

3 cups water

3 cups sugar

4 whole cloves

1 cinnamon stick

grated rind of half
   a lemon

1. Peel pears and place them in a bowl of cold water to prevent discoloring.

2. In a large saucepan, bring water, sugar, and juice to a boil. Add rind, cloves, and cinnamon stick.

3. Add pears and simmer slowly until fruit is tender, about half an hour. Pears should have a shiny look.

4. Remove pears with a slotted spoon to a shallow, flat-bottomed dish and allow to cool.

5. Trim bottoms of pears slightly so they can be placed in a standing position. Then pour some of the syrup over them and refrigerate for several hours.

CRÈME ANGLAISE

4 egg yolks

2 teaspoons cornstarch

6 tablespoons sugar

2 cups half-and-half

   1/8 teaspoon mace,
optional

1. Mix yolks, cornstarch, and sugar in top of a double boiler.

2. Scald half-and-half in separate saucepan and slowly add to egg mixture, stirring constantly. Cook over hot, but not boiling, water until sauce thickens.

3. Stir in mace if desired. Remove from heat, cover, and allow to cool. Chill thoroughly until ready to serve.

Yield: 6 servings

Marinated Fresh Figs

16 fresh ripe black figs

3 tablespoons crème
   de cacao

1-1/2 cups sour cream

1 tablespoon sweet cocoa
   or grated chocolate

1. Wash and drain figs. Cut in halves, or these may be prepared as whole figs rather than halves.

2. Stir crème de cacao into sour cream. Dip fig halves into flavored sour cream so that they are completely coated.

3. Refrigerate.

4. Sprinkle with cocoa or grated chocolate just before serving.

Sweet Pineapple Boats

2 ripe pineapples

*1 quart fresh
      strawberries, hulled*

1 cup heavy cream

1/2 cup maple syrup

*1/4 cup chopped walnuts
      or pecans*

additional maple syrup

1. Cut the pineapples in half lengthwise, leaving top attached to each half. With a curved sharp knife, cut around the inner edge of the pineapple and lift out the fruit. Remove and discard core. Then cut the pineapple meat into bite-sized cubes.

2. Wash and drain strawberries. Cut in halves and pile into the pineapple shells along with the pineapple cubes. Chill.

3. In a chilled bowl, beat cream and syrup until firm. Keep in refrigerator until ready to serve.

4. Just before serving sprinkle nuts on drained fruit and gently mix them through.

5. The fruit can be served from the boats into fruit dessert saucers. A bowl of plain maple syrup along with the bowl of maple whipped cream can be passed.

Yield: 8 servings

Another way of serving this fruit is to gently stir the maple whipped cream into the fruit and then serve. The extra bowl of maple syrup is nice for those who like the added sweet taste.

Apples Gratiné

7 medium cooking
    apples (about
    3 pounds)

1/4 cup butter

1 ten-ounce jar plum jam

3 tablespoons brandy

1/4 cup butter

1/2 cup granulated sugar

3 eggs, separated

2 tablespoons flour

2 teaspoons cinnamon

1 cup fresh rye bread
    crumbs (about 3-4
    slices

1/4 teaspoon salt

1/4 cup confectioners'
    sugar

Preheat oven to 325°F.

1. Peel and core apples and cut into lengthwise pieces about 1/4-inch thick.

2. Saute apple slices on both sides in butter until tender. As each layer is finished, turn it into a 9 × 9 × 2-inch buttered baking dish.

3. Warm plum jam and stir in brandy. Then pour it over apples.

4. Cream butter and sugar until fluffy. Add egg yolks, flour, cinnamon, and crumbs. Mix thoroughly.

5. Beat egg whites and salt until stiff. Fold into bread crumb mixture and spread evenly over apples.

6. Bake in oven for 15 to 20 minutes. Top will puff slightly. Then sprinkle it with sifted confectioners' sugar and bake for another 25 minutes, until it is a golden color.

7. Cool, cover, and refrigerate overnight.

Yield: about 6 servings

The flavors improve with refrigeration; however, this may be eaten warm. Another addition might be a cream sauce, whipped cream, or vanilla ice cream.

170

AMOR FRÍO

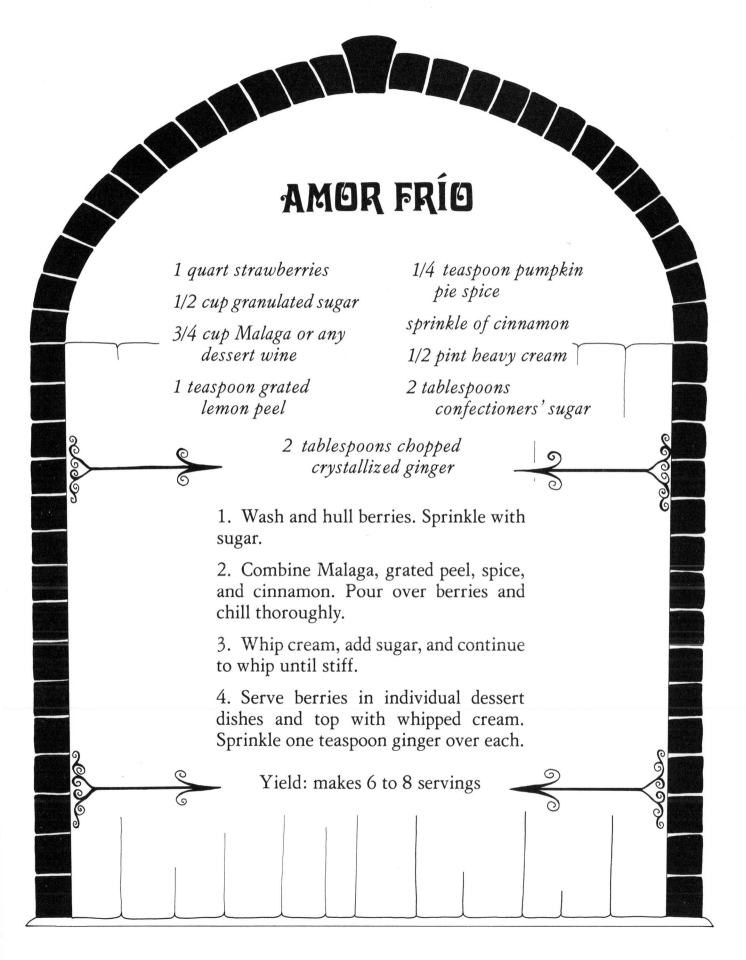

1 quart strawberries

1/2 cup granulated sugar

3/4 cup Malaga or any dessert wine

1 teaspoon grated lemon peel

1/4 teaspoon pumpkin pie spice

sprinkle of cinnamon

1/2 pint heavy cream

2 tablespoons confectioners' sugar

2 tablespoons chopped crystallized ginger

1. Wash and hull berries. Sprinkle with sugar.

2. Combine Malaga, grated peel, spice, and cinnamon. Pour over berries and chill thoroughly.

3. Whip cream, add sugar, and continue to whip until stiff.

4. Serve berries in individual dessert dishes and top with whipped cream. Sprinkle one teaspoon ginger over each.

Yield: makes 6 to 8 servings

Fleurs de Lily

MERINGUE LILIES

3 egg whites

1/2 cup sugar

1/3 cup sifted flour

1/3 cup finely ground almonds

1/3 cup butter, melted and cooled

1 teaspoon vanilla

Preheat oven to 400°F.

1. Beat egg whites until frothy. Gradually beat in sugar and continue to beat until stiff.

2. Carefully fold in sifted flour, ground almonds, melted butter, and vanilla.

3. Using 2 tablespoons dough for each lily, drop on a greased baking sheet 2 inches apart.

4. Bake until lightly browned for 8 to 10 minutes. Loosen with spatula and quickly form into little cones. Seal by overlapping edges. Cool.

FILLING

1/2 pint heavy cream

1 cup strawberries or blueberries

handful of pistachio nuts, ground

5. Beat heavy cream until stiff. Fold in sugar to taste. Clean and drain whatever fruit you choose. Fold into whipped cream and fill cones with fruit-flavored cream. Sprinkle with ground pistachio nuts.

Yield: makes 10 to 12 lilies.

This recipe was created by the chef of the Ritz in Paris, on the occasion of an appearance by opera singer Lily Pons.

South Sea Bananas

12 macaroons

8 ripe yellow bananas

1/2 cup melted butter

salt, white pepper and
   freshly grated
   nutmeg

1/2 cup apricot jam

1. Dry 12 macaroons in a 200°F. oven. Pulverize in blender.

Preheat oven to 350°F.

2. Select small bananas, uniform in size. Peel, cut in halves the long way and brush with melted butter.

3. Sprinkle each banana half with salt, pepper, and nutmeg.

4. Place in a lightly buttered shallow baking dish and bake for 10 minutes.

5. Warm apricot jam and strain through a sieve. When bananas are finished, roll each half in the strained jam and then in macaroon crumbs.

Yield: 8 servings

Caution should be taken not to overbake bananas or they will become mushy and difficult to handle. A topping of hard sauce or whipped cream may be added.

Lake Atitlan, about two hours away from Guatemala in Central America, is a beautiful, blue, blue lake with a rumbling volcano in full view. We stayed at the Hotel Atitlan right on the Lake and this was a popular dessert on the menu.

Brazilian Bananas with Coconut

6 ripe yellow bananas
of uniform size

1 tablespoon lemon
juice, strained

1/2 cup orange juice,
strained

1/4 cup brown sugar,
tightly packed

2 tablespoons butter

1 cup grated coconut

Preheat oven to 400°F.

1. Peel bananas and cut them in half lengthwise. Arrange the halves in a well-buttered baking dish. If the dish is too small to put all of the bananas in one layer, place them in layers. I prefer the layered arrangement.

2. Mix the lemon juice and orange juice with brown sugar and pour over the bananas.

3. Dot the surface of the bananas with butter and sprinkle the coconut over the entire top.

4. Bake for 12 to 15 minutes. The bananas should be soft and the coconut browned.

Yield: 6 servings

A soft custard sauce or even one of the commercial whips generously flavored with sherry, rum or an orange liqueur will add the final touch to this delightful Brazilian dessert.

Norwegian Red Fruit Pudding with Cream

1 pint fresh strawberries

1 pint fresh raspberries

2-1/2 tablespoons sugar

1 tablespoon cornstarch

2 tablespoons cold water

1/2 pint heavy cream

2 tablespoons sugar

1/2 teaspoon vanilla

1. Wash and hull berries and pat dry. Puree in blender. There should be about 2-1/2 cups.

2. Pour berry puree into a large saucepan, stir in sugar, and bring to a boil, stirring constantly.

3. Make a paste of cornstarch and water and stir into fruit mixture. Reduce heat and simmer until it thickens, stirring constantly. DO NOT BOIL.

4. Pour into large serving bowl or individual dessert dishes and chill for several hours before serving.

5. Beat cream until it begins to thicken. Add the sugar and vanilla. Cream should be just thick enough to show ripples, not stiff.

Yield: 6 servings

Cold Fruit Pudding
(Fruktsoppa, from Sweden)

2/3 cup dried apricots

2/3 cup dried prunes

6 cups water

1 stick cinnamon

2 lemon slices

1/4 cup sugar

1/4 cup raisins

1 tart apple, pared,
    cored and sliced

2 tablespoons cornstarch
    or potato starch

water

1/2 pint heavy cream,
    whipped, optional

1. Wash dried apricots and prunes and soak in cold water for half an hour.

2. Add cinnamon stick, lemon slices, and sugar. Simmer covered until almost tender, about 15 minutes, stirring occasionally.

3. Stir in raisins and apple and cook a few minutes longer.

4. Mix cornstarch with a little water to make a paste. Add to fruit mixture and cook until it becomes thick and clear.

5. Place fruit in serving bowl. Taste for flavor. More lemon juice or sugar may be added, depending on taste.

6. Chill and serve with whipped cream.

Yield: 4 servings

Flaming Cherries

1 sixteen-ounce can
 pitted black cherries

1 tablespoon cornstarch

1 tablespoon sugar

1 teaspoon lemon
 juice

1/2 cup warmed brandy

French vanilla ice cream

1. Drain cherries and reserve juice.

2. Combine cornstarch and sugar. Add a small amount of juice to make a paste. Then add balance of juice and simmer in a chafing dish or saucepan for several minutes, stirring constantly.

3. Add cherries and lemon juice; remove from heat.

4. Ignite brandy and pour over cherries.

5. Divide ice cream into individual portions and pour sauce over top.

Yield: makes 6 servings

Ingredient Substitutions

Ingredient Amount	Substitution
1 tablespoon flour, as thickener	½ tablespoon cornstarch, potato starch, arrowroot
1 cup all-purpose flour	1 cup unsifted all-purpose flour minus 2 tablespoons
1 cup sifted cake flour	7/8 cup sifted all-purpose flour or 1 cup minus 2 tablespoons sifted all-purpose flour
2 cups corn syrup	1 cup sugar plus ¼ cup liquid
1 cup honey	1¼ cups sugar plus ¼ cup liquid
1 ounce chocolate	3 tablespoons cocoa plus 1 tablespoon fat
1 cup butter	1 cup margarine or 7/8 to 1 cup hydrogenated fat plus ½ teaspoon salt
1 cup whole milk	½ cup evaporated milk plus ½ cup water, or ¼ cup sifted whole milk powder plus 7/8 cup water
1 cup coffee cream	7/8 cup milk plus 3 tablespoons butter
1 cup heavy cream	¾ cup milk plus 1/3 cup butter
1 cup buttermilk or sour milk	1 tablespoon vinegar or lemon juice plus enough sweet milk to make 1 cup; let stand 5 minutes
1 teaspoon baking powder	¼ teaspoon baking soda plus 5/8 teaspoon cream of tartar
1 medium lemon	2 to 3 tablespoons lemon juice
1 lemon	1 tablespoon grated lemon rind
1 medium orange	6 to 8 tablespoons orange juice

Table of Equivalents

3 teaspoons = 1 tablespoon
4 tablespoons = ¼ cup
8 tablespoons = ½ cup
16 tablespoons = 1 cup
1 cup = 8 fluid ounces
2 cups = 1 pint
4 cups = 1 quart
4 quarts = 1 gallon
2 tablespoons liquid = 1 ounce
½ cup liquid = ¼ pint

5 tablespoons flour = 1 ounce
1 cup flour = 4 ounces
1 tablespoon butter = ½ ounce
1 pound butter = 2 cups (4 sticks)
2 cups granulated sugar = 1 pound
4 cups confectioners' sugar = 1 pound
2¼ cups brown sugar (packed) = 1 pound
1 square baking chocolate = 1 ounce
15-ounce package raisins = 3 cups
1 cup nuts = about 4 ounces
1 pound nuts in the shell = about ½ pound nut meats
1 cup shredded coconut = about 3 ounces

1 kilogram = 2.2 pounds
1 pound = 454 grams
1 ounce = 28 grams

1 kilogram = 1000 grams
1 gram = 1000 milligrams
1 milligram = 1000 micrograms

A liter is a little more than a quart.
1 gallon = 3.79 liters
1 quart = .95 liter or 950 milliliters
1 pint = .48 liters or 480 milliliters
1 cup (8 fluid ounces) = .24 liters or 240 milliliters
1 tablespoon = 15 milliliters
1 teaspoon = 5 milliliters

R. Durand

Disclaimer

"Every time Goldye gains a pound, *we* go on a diet" says my husband. True. Another complaint from my loving partner is that the only time we have one of these luscious treats is when we have party guests. Right again. That's the way it is, and herein is my disclaimer on the subject of desserts being incompatible with good health. Did you imagine I can have a rich dessert every other day of my life and not put on weight? No way; even if he can, I cannot. Everyone is weight conscious and health-minded these days and as a nutritionist myself I never lose sight of the fact that excesses of any foodstuffs would be devastating. So here is reinforcement, should you need it: my special desserts are meant for your *special* occasions. The pièce de resistance to provide flourish and fanfare — not fat!

Goldye Mullen

THE MOOSEWOOD COOKBOOK
by Mollie Katzen. ". . . one of the most attractive, least dogmatic meat-less cookbooks printed . . . an engaging blend of hand lettered care and solid food information." —Bob Heisler, *The New York Post*
"If there is a 'new' American cooking, you will find it in *The Moose-wood Cookbook*." —Judith Huxley, Book World, *The Washington Post*. 8½ x 11" $7.95 paper, $9.95 cloth

HONEY FEAST
by Gene Opton and Nancie Hughes. Appetizers, meat and vegetable dishes, as well as the breads, sweets, and savories that honey has long been famous for. More than 100 recipes from around the world. $4.95 paper, $7.95 cloth

THE PRESBYTERIAN LADIES COOK BOOK
Facsimile of the original 1875 edition. Fascinating to read as well as to cook from, the recipes invite us into the homes and lives of our grand-parents. $4.95 paper

BACKPACKER'S COOKBOOK
Authors Margaret Cross and Jean Fiske, enthusiastic California back-packers themselves, provide valuable advice on pre-trip menu planning, on-the-trail nourishment, and food preparation. Illustrated. $3 paper.

GORMAN ON CALIFORNIA PREMIUM WINES
by Robert Gorman. "The first half is a primer on wines and wine-making, and useful indeed for one just starting out on connoisseur-manship, while the second half takes up each variety of wine—describing the grapes, the expected tastes, and the vineyards that produce them. A good and useful book." —Julia Child, in *The Boston Globe*. $5.95 paper, $8.95 cloth

At your local book store, or when ordering direct please add $.50 additional each paperback, or $.75 each clothbound for postage & handling.

TEN SPEED PRESS
BOX 7123, BERKELEY, CALIFORNIA 94707